The Hidden Edge

The Hidden Edge

Why Mental Fitness is the Only Advantage That Matters in Business

Jodie Rogers

WILEY

This edition first published 2021.

© 2021 by Jodie Rogers

 This work was produced in collaboration with Write Business Results Limited. For more information on Write Business Results' business book, blog, and podcast services, please visit their website: www.writebusinessresults .com, email us on info@ writebusinessresults.com or call us on 020 3752 7057.

Registered office
John Wiley & Sons Ltd, The Atrium, Southern Gate, Chichester, West Sussex, PO19 8SQ, United Kingdom

For details of our global editorial offices, for customer services and for information about how to apply for permission to reuse the copyright material in this book please see our website at www.wiley.com.

Wiley publishes in a variety of print and electronic formats and by print-on-demand. Some material included with standard print versions of this book may not be included in e-books or in print-on-demand. If this book refers to media such as a CD or DVD that is not included in the version you purchased, you may download this material at http://booksupport.wiley.com. For more information about Wiley products, visit www.wiley.com.

Designations used by companies to distinguish their products are often claimed as trademarks. All brand names and product names used in this book are trade names, service marks, trademarks or registered trademarks of their respective owners. The publisher is not associated with any product or vendor mentioned in this book.

Limit of Liability/Disclaimer of Warranty: While the publisher and author have used their best efforts in preparing this book, they make no representations or warranties with respect to the accuracy or completeness of the contents of this book and specifically disclaim any implied warranties of merchantability or fitness for a particular purpose. It is sold on the understanding that the publisher is not engaged in rendering professional services and neither the publisher nor the author shall be liable for damages arising herefrom. If professional advice or other expert assistance is required, the services of a competent professional should be sought.

Library of Congress Cataloging-in-Publication Data is Available:

ISBN 9781119807735 (hardback)
ISBN 9781119807759 (ebk)
ISBN 9781119807742 (epub)

Cover Design: Wiley

Set in 12/16pt, AGaramondPro by SPi Global, Chennai, India.

Printed and bound by CPI Group (UK) Ltd, Croydon CR0 4YY

C807735_270421

For my dad,

Peter Matthew Rogers:

May your soul and spirit fly into the mystic

CONTENTS

  8 Navigating Thinking Traps   97

  9 Fear Response and Neuroplasticity   109

Part Four **Limiting and Empowering Beliefs**   **115**

 10 The 'Rules' We Should Be Breaking   117

 11 How to Reframe Limiting Beliefs   139

Part Five **Values: Principles We Live By**   **145**

 12 Values and Decision Making   147

 13 Uncovering Your Values   163

 14 Using Values to Navigate Conflict   173

Part Six **Stress and Performance**   **181**

 15 Stress and Control   183

 16 Overcoming the Amygdala Hijack   189

 17 Flow Versus Frazzle   197

         Mental Fitness in Practice   217

         Conclusion   229

         Index   235

PREFACE

This book is the product of working inside and alongside businesses for the last 20 years. But it's not just my career experience that I've poured into the book, it's also my personal experience. I've seen what a lack of 'mental fitness' and even basic mental health can do to people. I grew up in a small fishing village in the north of Ireland where thinking about your thoughts, emotions, or behaviours was not a done thing (still isn't). I was a teenager during 'the troubles' where bombs and shootings were a routine part of life. Self-actualising, or any form of personal or professional development, was not generally on the top of people's lists, nor was mental and emotional well-being. But people fought, they believed that more was possible, that what you had wasn't all that there was. There was always hope.

My childhood was idyllic. My two brothers and I spent our days outside exploring, climbing trees, swimming in the sea, building makeshift huts, plotting against imaginary foes, inventing submarines, and flying go-karts. Yet, at the age of 11, I distinctly remember my twin brother, Johnny, slipping into a form of childhood depression which lasted for a year or so. There were many potentially contributing factors; reflecting on it today he believes it was because academically he was a square block being forced into a round hole. It was also the first year we had ever been separated (as I went to an all-girls secondary school at 11). The teacher who told him he was 'only good enough to build walls in the mountains' didn't help either. Small and not so small things can have a disproportionate impact on our life. One single comment can impact our belief in our capabilities and subsequently our performance, if we let it. But it was my parents' firm belief in him and his own inner resolve that saw him through that period.

My mum and our older brother Naithin were determined to find him something *practical* to focus on (none of us are what you would call 'natural academics'). Naithin discovered a film and photography course and, even though it was miles away, my mum drove Johnny there every day. It was this course that gave him a glimmer of hope, a chance to do something practical instead of theoretical like most of what is offered in academia. He flourished. Today he is one of the most successful people I know. He's a wildlife cameraman and has travelled the four corners of the world, working on natural history documentaries like *One Strange Rock*, *Earth's Natural Wonders*, and *Blue Planet* for the BBC, National Geographic, Discovery, Netflix, and Apple TV. You name it, he's done it. He could have easily fallen through the cracks. Many of my friends and family (including myself) have experienced a mental or emotional challenge at some point in our lives, one that has had an impact on how we show up in life and work. You have too.

How do I know? Because you have a mind, and you know very little about it. Besides, if you met someone who told you they had never ever had any form of physical illness in their life, not even a cold, would you believe them? Of course not. It's the same for our emotional and mental well-being. But I don't want to focus on how and where things go wrong. I want to focus on how and where we can set ourselves up for success.

I've spent much of my life in despair at how little is done to enhance, strengthen, and leverage our inner resources, and how little is even known by the general public about our 'inner game'. I'm on a mission to change that, because the knowledge, the exercises, and the tools all exist. They are just not easily accessible or packaged in a way that is engaging, practical and, dare I say it, enjoyable!

That changes with this book.

My business, Symbia (www.symbiapartners.com), has been working in this space for the last decade. We work with senior leaders and their teams at Unilever, Coca-Cola, L'Oréal, Mondelez, and many more. Our company vision is to positively impact the lives of one million people in the next 3yrs, and we are on track to achieve that. Everything we do is based on the belief that there is untapped potential in everyone. We are our own brakes and our own accelerators. I've spent years shaking and waking people up to their limiting beliefs, the thinking traps in their minds, the emotional patterns playing out in their lives. If we only knew a fraction as much about our minds as we do about our washing machines, we'd be laughing!

In this book, I've sought to curate and blend a number of schools of thought from neuropsychology, behavioural economics, emotional and social intelligence, positive psychology, and so on. I've packaged it in an 'easy-to-grasp' way and brought it to life with real-life case studies, data, anecdotes, and stories from my life and my work. My career began in qualitative and quantitative research; as such, I've interviewed tens of thousands of people over the last 20 years. Every project we work on for our clients starts with a diagnostic phase. Therefore, we have gathered a lot of insight and can see the macro patterns and trends playing out in the companies we work with. I've weaved that insight into the book so you can see how the viewpoints are validated.

It's worth saying though, that I'm not coming to you as an expert, I'm here as a fellow human. I'm championing Mental Fitness because I truly believe in it, because I've had to practise it and rely on it as a way of life. Like you, I'm not immune to life's challenges; life throws us all curveballs, no one can change that. It's how we respond to them that matters.

I've had a pretty good life: the daughter of art teachers, a decent education, and an idyllic childhood: the sea outside my front door, mountains outside my back door. I've travelled the world for adventure and for work. There have been ups and downs, but nothing like 2020.

Like most, my business was affected. Clients postponed workshops, cancelled team sessions, or just completely disappeared as they dealt with the impact of COVID-19. I had a team to support in a time of crisis. My husband's business and income vanished overnight. We live in Spain, so we were in an extreme lockdown situation; no daily exercise for us. There were helicopters in the sky and police patrolling the streets (which reminded me of Belfast in the old days). My two-year-old and four-and-a-half-year-old were not allowed outside of our apartment walls for 45 days. Trying to run a business with two little people with intense cabin fever was enough to impact anyone's stress levels and performance.

But the hardest part of 2020 wasn't any of this.

In January, my dad was diagnosed with cancer. He passed away in May, when we were all still in lockdown. I couldn't get back to Ireland to see him. If he had passed away at any other moment in his 73 years of life I would have been by his side.

2020 kicked my ass, but I kicked its ass back.

What happens to us rarely kills us; it's the story we tell ourselves about what happens that takes us down.

It's easy to stay focused on the 'car crash'; we're designed that way.

The negativity bias insists we pay attention to the negative things because they could be threats to our survival. We therefore need to consciously make an effort to see the positive things that are in plain sight.

This year, I could get lost in the negative story – if I shared it, people would sympathise – but it doesn't serve me. Although my business was affected by the pandemic, we have bounced back, our team has doubled, and we've brought on five more major corporate clients. The crisis gave us laser focus. We're busier than ever (businesses are finally realising the importance of mental *fitness* in playing the long game). My goal for the year was to travel less, move some of my business online, and spend more time with my kids. I didn't want a pandemic to deliver it, but mission accomplished all the same. I've also finally birthed the book that has been inside of me for the last seven years – there's a lot to be proud of, yet it's easily missed.

So, my mission with this book is for you to take away one key insight, exercise, anecdote, or tool that will positively affect your life – although I'm confident you'll take away much more than one. With everything that I share I've also shown how to apply it to teams because this is the work myself and my team do every day at Symbia.

I truly believe that we all have untapped potential within us. When we work on and enhance our 'mental fitness', we unlock possibilities in ourselves and in our teams that we didn't know were there.

ACKNOWLEDGEMENTS

Thank you to my family and friends and everyone who contributed to this book and to the friends, colleagues, and clients who let me brainstorm and experiment with them. A special thank you to everyone who took part in my interviews: Tim Munden, Marcus Hunt, Nathalie Slechte, Dr David Wilkinson, Shawn Conway, Mathew McCarthy, and Aldo Kane, and our financial services clients, who all provided excellent insight on the topic of mental fitness in business and in life, bringing new voices and different perspectives to the book.

Tim Munden, you deserve mentioning twice. I'm immensely grateful for the work you are driving on the inner game in Unilever. Thank you for trusting me and my company Symbia as a partner on this important journey. I am extremely grateful to Stan Sthanunathan and Gemma Bumpstead of Unilever who were pioneers in bringing mental fitness into the Consumer & Market Insights (CMI) function and honoured us with permission to include the case study at the back of this book.

A special thank you to Ann Suvarnapunya for creating all the images for the book and being heavily involved in all of our Mental Fitness offerings at Symbia. Also, thank you to Suzy Hegg, whose brilliantly analytical brain was a great support when creating the Mental Fitness business case.

To friends, colleagues, and clients of Symbia who have trusted us with their leaders and teams around the world, we thank you for the partnership and the opportunity to have a positive impact on your people.

Gratitude to Georgia Kirke and Kat Lewis, who have skilfully navigated the minefield of mental fitness and expertly helped shape it into the book it is today.

Many thanks to Annie Knight and all of the Wiley team who helped turn a major life and business goal into a reality.

Last, but always first, to my husband, Johnny Nunes, and our two boys, Theo and Finn. How you created space for me to write this book during a global pandemic is a mystery, but I am eternally grateful for your never-ending support. You always said you were my number one believer – I know that's the truth because I've felt it every step of the way. To infinity and beyond ;-)

INTRODUCTION

The book's title, *The Hidden Edge, Why Mental Fitness is the Only Advantage That Matters in Business*, is deliberately provocative. I felt it was important to ignite debate. Too often we just default to external factors being prioritised in business, budget, business plans, investment, market dynamics, and so on. These matter – of course they do – but they are not as important as the people who sit behind them. If we want businesses that are agile and adaptable to change, we first need people who are. Flexible business models are meaningless if we don't also have agile mindsets and behaviours. Your people are your business's most important asset. If we want resilient businesses, we must build resilient teams, and to do this we need to empower them with the knowledge and tools to understand and leverage *their* most important asset – their minds. This book is the first step.

When athletes are training, they know that success is dependent upon more than just their physical performance – their mindset, i.e. staying focused, motivated, and confident, has a critical role to play. This is often referred to as their 'mental game' or 'inner game'.

We all have an inner game. It refers to everything that goes on in our minds: our thinking patterns, our emotional regulation, beliefs, mindset, and so on. It's a combination of these factors that drives our decisions and influences the outcomes in our lives.

Much like physical fitness, the strength of our inner game – our 'mental fitness' – varies throughout our lives and is equally something we have to work at.

Just as we exercise our muscles to become stronger, through focus and practice we can modify and strengthen our mindset and thinking style to help us bounce back from the setbacks and challenges that come our way. In business, the level of mental fitness in the individuals who make up your organisation is your business's 'hidden edge'. In other words, mental fitness is a competitive advantage in business.

Negative thinking patterns play a significant role in depression and anxiety. If we make no attempt to work on them, our ability to self-regulate diminishes, our emotional resilience becomes fragile, and, overall, our mental fitness suffers. Whether we are talking at the level of organisations, teams or the individuals within them, when 'mental fitness' suffers, so does performance.

It's important not to weaken our mental fitness but, equally, we need to be putting in effort to **enhance** it. Being more aware of our thinking style – and using techniques to avoid thinking traps and manage self-limiting beliefs – gives us more control over how we respond to the events and situations in our lives.

Our minds are our most important asset. But do we take time to look after them? Have you ever stopped to notice your thought patterns? Are you aware of the effect they're having on your life?

The ways we think about ourselves or the world can help us or get in our way, support or harm our health, enable or inhibit our success at work and in our relationships. Our inner game can play for us or against us – it can hold us back or propel us forward. So, the question is: Have you mentally set yourself up for success? Are you and your team 'mentally fit' and prepared for the challenges ahead?

If you can master your thinking and your mindset, you can release confidence and potential within your employees that they didn't even know was there. It's this that will amplify their personal presence and impact both in life and in work. It is this that will keep them flexible and creative in the face of uncertainty.

The challenge is that most of us have not been taught this. The education system doesn't have it as a topic on the curriculum. Unless you are working in the field, have a natural curiosity for the topic or have found yourself in therapy at some point, it's unlikely that you have come across both the knowledge and the tools necessary to navigate and influence your cognitive and emotional experience of the world.

This is why it's such an important topic. People aren't naturally learning about it, and there's no mandatory reading, which seems ridiculous when you think about it because there absolutely should be!

And this lack of understanding shows up in companies of all sizes, industries, and locations all around the world. I've worked with leaders and their teams in countries on every continent across the globe over the course of the last decade. I've helped companies in industries from fast-moving consumer goods (FMCG) to aviation, finance to telecommunications, entertainment to marketing, supply chain, R&D functions, and many more. I've worked up and down the food chain with everyone from interns to CEOs. Irrespective of the many variables that set one company apart from another, I have observed the same set of blind spots in all of them when it comes to mental fitness.

The first is that leaders come to me with a multitude of culture- and business-related goals and challenges that they think they need help addressing, but they are not usually the ones that really do need addressing. Companies do not always diagnose their issues correctly to begin with before settling on a solution, and so, the wrong things repeatedly get addressed. Or at least, the real issues are not being tackled and therefore continue to fester.

For example, leaders will often say of their organisational challenges:

'We need to increase productivity!'

'We need to refresh our strategy.'

'We need to define roles and responsibilities.'

'We have to create a "ways of working" manifesto,' and so on.

Indeed, these may be the outcomes they seek, and they are possible to achieve, but they are not enough on their own to ensure ongoing productivity, happiness, and creativity from everyone throughout the organisation at every level. Because they are all tangible and visible, whereas we need to equally explore what lies underneath these. What beliefs, values, and mindsets are within the people working towards the business goals? If I were to take every brief of this nature at face value, I could deliver exactly to such expectations as the ones listed above, and the clients would be happy upon delivery, but their challenges wouldn't be resolved.

Here are the four fundamental reasons why:

- The person who perceives the team's challenges and has the authority to act on them and do something about them is usually a leader. By the very nature of their position, they don't fully know what is actually happening 'on the floor'. It's much like when parents of teenagers don't have the full picture (and I'm not saying company executives are like teenagers). It's simply human nature to shield details from those in authority.

- By focusing on the assumed best solution – for example, the new strategy, organisational chart, roles, and responsibilities – there is an underlying assumption that the 'problem' presented is the right one to be solving.

- Briefs for change created by leaders, usually, unwittingly, work on the 'symptom' level and rarely seek to uncover the 'cause', because the symptoms are confused *as being* the cause.

- In the fast-paced world that we work in, results and outcomes are favoured over process. This means that the time in the journey from current Point A to desired Point B is crunched to accelerate outcomes. Because of this, the outcomes are diluted and often superficial. I find that the more energy and focus are invested in the 'how' (the journey from uncovering the underlying cause to introducing solutions), the better, more impactful, and longer lasting the results, every time.

Team and company leaders' perceived challenges are valid. They are very valuable indeed. But they must be considered as just one input. Other valid perspectives on the real issues with teams and culture also include those of each member of the board, leadership team, wider team and people who work with the team.

Only with that complete bigger picture and a view of the teams 'inner game' can you start to build a view of the mental fitness levels within your company, separate symptoms from cause, and know where to focus your energy. You can then point at core problems, reframe them and do the work to really know which challenges need to be solved first. More often than not, core problems are not always immediately visible, because they are at a mindset level. Therefore, seeking to work on both the visible and invisible obstacles to performance can be a game changer for any team.

Mental fitness is grounded in emotional and social intelligence, and it's this insight that then prepares us to embrace change, be resilient in the face of setbacks, and effectively manage emotions, ambitions, and behaviour. It's a journey, one of self-discovery and awareness, and one which can (and does) take years.

In the following chapters, I seek to show you how and why this insight matters. I will demonstrate how small but significant changes to your perception, thinking, and mindset can make a difference to how you experience, and subsequently show up in, life and business. My intention is to demystify the workings of the mind by sharing some basic neuroscience and behavioural psychology and showing you how to use this knowledge to unlock behavioural change within yourself and your teams.

I encourage you to read this book with yourself in mind first; play with the subject matter and complete the exercises for yourself. In doing so, you'll see the power that small tweaks to your perception, thinking, and belief systems have to completely change your experience of life. Once you've experienced this insight first-hand, take it to your teams and to your organisation. I have a number of ways I can support you in this, which you can find at www.symbiapartners.com.

A word of caution though: the temptation is to think 'I know this', and it's true that there's a chance you will have come across some of the thinking I'm going to share with you in different ways at different times. But here's the thing: are you actively using this knowledge to help you manage the stresses and pressures of business and work life? Have you applied the understanding to help you navigate conflict? Is it being leveraged to enhance confidence? Are you using it to help yourself out of 'thinking traps' and self-criticism? Are you applying it to get the best out of your teams? Are you actively using your values to make decisions that are both right for you and for your business? Knowing (or simply having heard something before) is not enough. Changing your behaviour because of what you know, is.

Most boards consider any topics related to our inner world (emotional, social, mental) the 'soft skills' that are distracting from what really matters – business metrics and results. But it is the wise and empathetic leaders who know that these skills are the real skills that matter. Empowering your people to leverage their most important asset, their own minds, is fundamentally the best investment any company can make.

If you told me you'd read 500 books about how to fly a plane, I still wouldn't get in a plane with you in the cockpit. The mistake many of us make is that we stop at *knowing*. This book is designed to encourage application.

As a result, I have made sure to include a variety of exercises throughout the book. These have all been trialled and tested in our workshops over the past decade, so I know them to be effective. You can also access further electronic resources here: www.symbiapartners .com/mentalfitnessresources.

I don't want this book to be a complete workbook, but I do want you to begin applying what you're learning as you're reading. This book, however, doesn't sit alone. It supports my Mental Fitness live workshops (which I've been running in corporate organisations since 2016), my interactive webinars (for a variety of clients including Coca-Cola, Peet's Coffee, and L'Oréal), and my successful Mental Fitness online course, which (in various bespoke versions) has already been implemented with great success in Unilever, Jacobs Douwe Egberts, and a prominent global bank – so you're in good company. If you want to learn more about this work, you can visit www .symbiapartners.com.

But for now, settle in, suspend your assumptions, biases, and beliefs, open your mind, and be willing to think differently.

For most people to have their wellbeing enhanced, they want support when they need it. This is why, in successful organisations, I've seen wellbeing moved from being a token about having medical insurance or gym membership to being truly practical: what can I receive today to make my job easier? What allows me to perform better? What allows me to switch off so I can have family time? When your company gives you the resources that actually help you be better, that's what makes the difference.

— *Marcus Hunt, Head of Global Health Services, EMEA, Johnson & Johnson*

Part One
Leadership and the Hidden Edge

In this first part of the book, I'll explain exactly what mental fitness is and how it is different from mental health and mental wellness. Mental fitness is very much focused on *strengthening* and *enhancing* our inner game for performance, and anyone can practice it.

We're also going to dive into the details of the cost of failing to do work in this space, as well as the benefit to individuals, businesses, and society if we invest time, energy, and money in empowering people with the knowledge and practice to work on their mental fitness.

Having spent the last 20 years working in and with businesses all over the world, I know that the best way to make a case with a leader is on business terms, which is why I've spent time building a business case for investing in mental fitness, which you'll find in Chapter 2. A more comprehensive version is available for download at www.symbiapartners.com/mentalfitnessresources. We've also gone beyond the conceptual and provided a real-life case study of what happened when 300 people within Unilever went through our programme. This case study appears at the back of the book.

This has been designed for anybody who wants to present the business case in their company. We've done the work for you; please do take it and use it. It will allow you to highlight why it's fundamentally important to invest in the minds and hearts of the people in your organisation. You have to remember that your people are your biggest assets, but within them their minds and their hearts are their biggest assets. These are largely untapped inner resources which represent a competitive edge for your business.

In Chapter 3, I paint a picture of what the world would be like if we all took the time to invest in our mental fitness, and how that would impact decision making, clarity, focus, and performance under stress.

1 Under the Skin of Leaders and Their Teams

C ompanies of all shapes and sizes have comprehensive and varied strategic plans, a multitude of business objectives across markets and sometimes industries – enough to keep the most efficient and driven executives continuously busy.

But if you were to distil the objectives of most global companies (decent companies with ethics, anyway) into just two areas, they would simply be:

- To drive revenue, profit, and growth
- To look after their people

In times of crises or uncertainty, these goals become even sharper. In times of stability and calm, they are in cohesion with each other. Unfortunately, in times of challenge, they are often in tension, if not in direct conflict, with each other. They become a paradox that leaders need to navigate, a polarity to be managed.

During the years that followed the economic crisis of 2008, when many companies were facing business challenges, and of course during the global pandemic of 2020, leaders expressed deep concern for their teams and guilt about the things they were being asked to deal with.

The pressure to recover revenue or 'recession-proof' a business inevitably has a personal impact on the workforce. No matter which way we cut it, we often unconsciously forgo our well-being in the pursuit of revenue. In times of challenge, an urgency and intensity builds up around scenario planning, rewriting strategy, data crunching, and forecasting endlessly in an attempt to predict an unpredictable future.

During the lockdown of 2020, one corporate leader told me, 'I can't wait to go back to the office so I can work less.' It was said in jest, but, like all good jokes, relies on some truth to be funny. This didn't come from a lazy person or a procrastinator. In fact, it came from a senior leader who was working around the clock and close to burnout.

I understand it. When Europe started locking down due to COVID-19, I had several conversations with leaders on what they were about to face. Looking after their people while mitigating revenue loss had become the paradoxical challenge at the forefront of their minds. As we continue to face into and plan for an uncertain world, this challenge needs to be managed skilfully and thoughtfully.

In an article by Sheryl Sandberg (COO, Facebook) and Rachel Thomas (Co-Founder, Lean In), published during the height of the first COVID-19 lockdown in May 2020, they said:

> *Only 40% of employees say their companies have taken steps to increase flexibility since the pandemic began, and fewer than 20% say their employer has rejiggered priorities or narrowed the scope of their work. That's not enough. Leaders and managers should move any deadline that can be moved, take a second look at targets set before the pandemic, rethink the timing of performance reviews, and remove low-priority items from the to-do list.*[1]

---

[1] Sandberg, S. and Thomas, R. (2020) 'The coronavirus pandemic is creating a "double double shift" for women. Employers must help', *Fortune* <https://fortune.com/2020/05/07/coronavirus-women-sheryl-sandberg-lean-in-employers-covid-19/>

But the truth is, the deadlines that can't be moved, the targets that can't be adjusted, and the ever-growing to-do lists are part of the stark reality that teams and business will be dealing with for the foreseeable future as we move into a faster-moving future and an increasingly unpredictable world.

So, while as leaders we may not have much control over deadlines and targets, what we DO have control over is how we can help our teams respond to and take on such gargantuan challenges.

And it's not just for times of heightened uncertainty like an economic crisis or a pandemic. The reality is that adaptability is one of the most important skills of the future. Actually, it always has been. As Charles Darwin pointed out, it's not the strongest species that survive but those most adaptable and responsive to change. That includes us humans, too.

Change used to take a long time to fully occur, certainly regarding how humans have lived on Earth. We were hunter-gatherers for several million years. We then moved to an agricultural way of life which lasted 12 000 years. The Industrial Age lasted only 100 years, and now we find ourselves in the Information Age, which has only been underway for a few decades, and several consultancies (including Deloitte and Boston Consulting Group) are already predicting the 'future of work', also known as the 'Augmented Age', could be upon us in less than 10 years.

The world and its workforce are changing at the fastest rate in history and will continue to do so. We therefore need to prepare our people to be agile in the face of that change. That requires mental flexibility, emotional regulation, self-awareness, and stress management, among a number of other competencies, which just aren't being prioritised enough.

In an increasingly complex and uncertain world, we all need tools to understand and manage our most important asset – our own minds – because it's our minds that act as our brakes and our accelerators. As we face into the new world, we need to consider how we respond to change. Rarely is change actually a problem; the problem is our natural human resistance to it.

We resist it because change breeds uncertainty, uncertainty brings doubt, which leads to hesitation and increases the risk of death – change and uncertainty generally have not been good for survival. Therefore, humans have been programmed to avoid them. But the world is different; we don't have the predators we used to, we can also navigate uncertainty and change more skilfully if we know how to acknowledge and live beside the anxiety and fear they often bring (knowing they most likely won't lead to death).

We need to be fine-tuning our minds to be more mentally agile and prepared for the long game. We need to be strengthening our neural pathways like we train our muscles at the gym. We need to be flexing our resiliency and preparing for the road ahead. We need to be getting our people mentally fit and empowering them to create their futures and that of the businesses and brands they represent. That's what this book sets out to support: empowering you and your people to enhance their own inner capabilities to navigate and flourish within a world of change. Because this is where true competitive advantage lives.

What is Mental Fitness?

When I talk about mental fitness as a concept, I focus on strengthening and enhancing – as such it can be seen as preventative in approach.

In the 1970s the healthcare system in the UK published a variety of reports emphasising the importance of a preventative approach to health. In Spring 1976, the government published 'Prevention and Health: Everybody's Business', a discussion paper that outlined 'a reassessment of public and personal health'. It argued that one potential solution to the problems then facing the National Health

Service (NHS) was a shift from a curative service to one that promoted health instead.[2]

While the idea of prevention wasn't completely new, it acquired a fresh urgency during this decade. Virginia Berridge notes that:

> [b]y the 1970s, a new style of public health was emergent, both nationally within the UK and internationally as well … [which] stressed the role of individual prevention and responsibility for health, with its roots in the earlier 1950s epidemiological 'paradigm shift' epitomized by smoking and lung cancer. The concept of the 'risk-avoiding individual' replaced the mass vaccination campaign image of 1950s public health.[3]

There was a realisation that, along with focusing on ridding the world of disease and illness, if society also spent energy and money on educating people to eat well, exercise, take vitamins, stop smoking, etc. they could keep millions out of the healthcare system and save billions, and many people would have a much richer quality of life. I believe passionately that we need to take the same attitude to mental health as we have done for physical health. We shouldn't focus all of our energy on just one side of the spectrum: illness. We should be investing in our own mental fitness and that of our teams – because that is where untapped potential lies (see Figure 1.1).

Figure 1.1 The Mental Fitness Spectrum.

[2]Clark, P. (2020, August) '"Problems of Today and Tomorrow": Prevention and the National Health Service in the 1970s', *Social History of Medicine*, 33 (3): 981–1000.

[3]Berridge, V. (2003) 'Post-war Smoking Policy in the UK and the Redefinition of Public Health', *Twentieth Century British History*, 14: 73.

We've all heard of mental illness; it's a taboo topic, and if you're dealing with mental illness within your teams (like burnout, depression, or anxiety), you're working at the 'cure' phase. It's extremely important to support people needing help. This phase generally leads to focusing on problems and solutions, getting people back to a place of 'wellness', rather than strengthening and enhancing people's mental fitness.

Even when discussing mental health, people often still think of ill health, and many glaze over, thinking, 'It doesn't apply to me, I don't have any problems.' The tendency is to think a mental health session means they're going to be 'assessed', or worse, they're going to be encouraged to meditate! The issue with the term 'mental health' is that many believe they are fine as long as they are not 'ill'.

The absence of illness does not equal health.

It's true that many companies have wellness or well-being teams, which largely focus on keeping people out of the 'illness' phase with some, but limited, focus on encouraging and enhancing 'fitness'. We can expect preventative approaches in the form of encouraging exercise, healthy eating, sleep, and meditation. All of these are absolutely important, they are foundational – but I believe there's more, much more.

What's missing is a proactive approach to *increasing* and *enhancing* mental fitness that is interesting, engaging, practical, and applicable both in life and in business.

If you can educate, inspire, and empower employees to look after their own mental fitness, besides the well-being benefits, the impact on individual performance, engagement, employee retention, and the bottom line is untold. Well, in fact, we know the impact because we've measured it. In this book, we have given you both a business case for why this matters and how it impacts the bottom line. We've also created a case study (on Unilever, at the end of the book) so you can see what is possible when you bring mental fitness into your business.

This book, and my work, aim to make significant strides towards changing our perspective. I want to move away from focusing only on one side of the spectrum – illness (a cure-focused mentality) and wellness – to also putting energy into the other end of the spectrum – fitness (an enhancing, strengthening, and empowering mentality to growth). Just as we go to the gym to exercise, to strengthen our heart and our bodies to get physically fit, we want people to be putting the same effort into their mental fitness, upfront and early. It is this work that creates a resilient workforce, adaptable in the face of change, agile when dealing with uncertainty, and creative when solving challenges and inevitable setbacks.

I want to help get your people mentally fit, to be prepared to play the long game in business and life. That means not waiting until there are tell-tale signs of fatigue, conflict, or reduced productivity, but working with people when they're 'okay' or 'fine' and getting them to 'strong' and 'great' – because this is how we unlock performance.

If Mental Fitness is 'the Hidden Edge' of Business, How Can It Be Harnessed?

We can do this by empowering people with the knowledge and tools to consciously navigate their thinking, regulate their emotions, manage stress, and skilfully handle uncertainty. The work I do focuses on enhancing people's overall emotional and social intelligence by teaching them how the mind works (and plays tricks on us), identifying and observing our default cognitive and emotional states (and the actions and behaviours they influence), and practising the tools and techniques necessary to optimise their inner world and in turn optimise their experience of the outer world.

Why does this matter? It matters because we aren't being taught this stuff. It's not in the curriculum, and our education system isn't tackling it to the degree it should. I work with leaders and their teams all over the world, across all types of industries and functions, all the way up and down the food chain. The truth is that most of them are ignoring the 'inner game', and uncertainty, emotions, and imposter syndrome are leaking out all over the place. There is a belief that there is no room for emotions in business, but as long as we are human there will be emotions; it's what we do with them that matters. Many of the execs we work with can't even fully describe how they're feeling, never mind know what to do with these feelings. That's why you can have people losing it in boardrooms and panicking in meetings. Most of them have just never learned the mental fitness basics, let alone the skills to help them better manage their experience of the world.

'Mental fitness' leverages emotional and social intelligence to enhance overall work and life performance. It empowers people to strengthen their psychological agility, emotional regulation, mindset, and resilience, making them higher performing and more adaptable in the face of challenge and change.

We know from numerous studies that emotional intelligence leads to a better ability to manage our emotions (emotion regulation) and that it is this ability to recognise (emotional literacy) and manage or regulate emotions which leads to better mental health outcomes (less stress, depression, negative thinking). This positive mental health leads both directly and indirectly to better work performance over time. We know this, so we now need to leverage it and train for it.[4]

Over the years, I've learned that companies face many challenges, and most of them are externalised; we point to tangible issues outside of us. But the truth is that the challenge for companies and their teams is often inside of us and *always human*.

---

[4]Devonish, D. (2016) 'Emotional Intelligence and Job Performance: The Role of Psychological Well-Being', *International Journal of Workplace Health Management*, 9 (4): 428–442.

Companies, organisations, businesses, teams: what are they, in their most basic form? They are simply a collection of humans, with all the emotions, thoughts, doubts, insecurities, and biases that come with being human. A big part of what drives human nature is fear. We are programmed to have a fight or flight response to fear as, historically, it's how we've survived.

That evolutionary programming is still behind our modus operandi today. It dictates our ability to respond to change, take risks, and manage uncertainty. In the workplace, as within any group setting, there are hierarchies and social systems that govern who does and says what.

It's the subtleties within these hierarchies that can often create tension. When tackling problems, some people shy away from pointing fingers at themselves or others for fear of 'being ostracised'. Others are afraid to expose their own vulnerabilities and shortcomings, should they be thought of as weak. We all tolerate situations that we're not fully comfortable with at times, just to keep the peace. As a result, it takes a carefully managed strategy to force change.

It takes courage to identify an issue, diagnose it correctly, and assume responsibility for our role in effective change. When things start to go wrong in teams, it is, in fact, far easier to point at something external as being at fault: the strategy, inefficient budgets, resource issues, the economy. They are tangible, but they often overlook the human element.

It is necessary to focus on what it means to be human if you want to be effective in business. That's true now, in a post-pandemic virtual world, more than ever before. The reality is that the most important work you will ever do within your company is deeply human and involves working on our collective 'mental fitness': the emotions, thoughts, and mindsets of the people making decisions.

When we go the extra mile to understand the human behind the strategies, the hopes, fears, ambitions, and insecurities, we are able to get under the skin of what's really going on in the ecosystem of our teams. Having worked as a qualitative researcher for many years, my preferred approach to uncover this insight is to have one-on-one, in-depth discussions with leaders and their teams before any type of intervention.

Taking this approach to team effectiveness creates four key benefits:

- I know exactly what is going on within the company, which gives me an authority and an edge when facilitating team sessions. This is particularly useful when we meet inevitable resistance, denial, or excuses – all of which are natural human defences.

- I can uncover what beliefs, values, and mindsets might be enabling or hampering a team's performance.

- We can then design a *deeper* session that will actually focus on what matters, make a measurable difference, and get the desired results.

- By 'saying the unsaid' – giving voice to the unexpressed challenges that have been creating drag in the team – we put everyone on the same page.
  - Unexpressed issues usually arise because either people couldn't pinpoint the problem in the first place or didn't want to raise the issue for fear of being seen as 'not a team player', or worse, losing their jobs. Giving voice to the 'unsaid' creates a combined sense of relief, safety, and motivation to solve the issues.

Pointing at the elephant in the room means you can finally begin to work on it.

In the hundreds of workshops my team and I have run across the world, 80% of what we do is spent working on the 'mental game' of business. It's spent helping teams understand what makes each of the individuals within them tick, how they problem-solve, respond to setbacks, manage stress, handle emotion, navigate their thinking, and deal with conflict. It's this deeper work that always makes the difference.

The temptation when working with teams is, of course, to work on teams. Generally, my clients want a jam-packed agenda where lots of 'work' is done as a collective to 'move the needle' or 'create momentum'. But if you do not work at the individual level first, the team efforts will be futile. I call this working on the 'me' before the 'we'.

That doesn't mean you spend months doing one-to-one coaching; not at all. You can work at the individual level while simultaneously working on the group. This is where the greatest shifts among my clients come from. But ignoring the complexities of what it means to be human means you will never be able to get a team functioning effectively.

Often this work begins when teams have come to me already facing challenges. It's rare that a team comes to me 'firing on all cylinders' and wanting to enhance things to the next level.

That's understandable; it's human nature to wait for a certain level of pain before taking action.

But what if you didn't have to wait for challenges and issues to appear before you 'did the work'? What if you could get ahead of yourself and have a prevention and enhancement approach rather than always having to pay out in time, money, and energy trying to fix or cure? What could that unlock among your people?

Some of the more progressive companies out there have started to realise the importance of enhancement over cure. Unilever is one of these core companies that is trail-blazing the way and has heavily invested in training and education around the idea of the 'inner game', because they are fully aware of the importance of investing in the personal development of their people, and empowering them to understand and navigate their own inner world to unlock business growth.

When you have mentally and emotionally healthy people ('mentally fit' people), you have resilient and agile teams. When you have resilient and agile teams, you have a healthy and agile business. And when you have a healthy business, it affects the bottom line positively. The work that I do with companies, whether it's leadership work, team sessions, designing programmes for central L&D (learning and development) teams, or taking full functions through learning journeys, is underpinned by my 'mental fitness' philosophy, which I will explain more about shortly.

But not all companies have realised this secret. Many are yet to understand that the hidden edge of business lies in the 'mental fitness' of your people, and that this is the most overlooked competitive advantage in the marketplace.

In truth, some do know it and either can't access the knowledge they need to act on it or have dismissed it for the more tangible initiatives they can sell in and get easier stakeholder buy-in for. That's not a criticism; we all know how difficult it is to convince people of the importance of such topics, especially when it feels like swimming upstream. Nine times out of 10, what's missing for corporate leaders who wish to dedicate time, money, and energy into figuring this out in their organisation is something measurable and tangible: numbers, metrics, return on investment (ROI). The following chapter presents hard-to-access statistics and financial data on the cost of ignoring mental fitness in organisations, and builds the business case to incorporate the concept of mental fitness into your organisation's culture and strategy for growth. I encourage you to use this business case in your company to persuade key decision-makers to invest in mental fitness. As such, we've made the business case available for download at www .symbiapartners.com/mentalfitnessresources.

I think working together with you [Jodie] has definitely opened my eyes to the importance of teaching people to look after their mental health and treat it as a key asset, something to be enhanced, through the lens of mental fitness. It's something that will help employees be successful in their careers and in their lives more generally. It's a simple but quite profound insight that mental fitness is something you need to work at in the same way you need to work on physical fitness, and ebbs and flows through your life.

— Head of Wellbeing, Global Financial Services

In 2020, the door got kicked open to discuss these topics and I always say that the time to change things is when things are changing. You [Jodie] brought this forward in a structured way with words like mental fitness, which could be scary, and turned that into something that ended up being a relief. You were meeting people where they were. It was great, because I think one of the most powerful things about the way that it was introduced into Peet's was the work to make sure that you and your team were meeting us where we were. We have a very smart group of people and they can understand, but you allowed us to feel it and that difference made a huge impact.

— Shawn Conway, CEO, Peet's Coffee

2 The Business Case for Investing in Mental Fitness

I n this chapter, I build a case for how mental fitness contributes to the bottom line in any organisation. Based on data from a variety of sources, it can be a valuable tool for HR and well-being practitioners or managers who need to make the case in their own organisations.

The World Health Organization (WHO) defines good mental health as follows:

'A state of wellbeing in which every individual realises his or her own potential, can cope with the normal stresses of life, can work productively and fruitfully, and is able to make a contribution to her or his community.'

In other words, good mental health isn't just the absence of ill health, just as good physical health isn't the absence of disease. Many arguments have been made (and often fallen on deaf ears) for the importance of addressing mental illness in the workplace and enhancing well-being.

This work is foundational and fundamentally important. But there is another opportunity here. What if we went beyond illness and wellness and also began to call for a focus on mental fitness in the workplace? As laid out in the last chapter, being *mentally fit* is about strengthening and enhancing, and just as peak physical fitness might see you through a marathon, peak mental fitness can help people to achieve extraordinary things – to become adaptable, more engaged, more resilient, and more creative in their work. With those sorts of results, why isn't everyone doing it?

Well, because the whole topic of 'mental' anything is largely still taboo. But beyond that, it's intangible in many ways. How do we know if we are doing it right? How can we convince stakeholders to invest in something we can't really measure? What IS the ROI? Do we know how it affects the bottom line? Is there a business case that lays out all the facts and figures in a simple, digestible way that I can use to first convince myself, then convince my company? Well, the answer is YES – this is it. In this book, we give you the executive summary version. If you want to access the comprehensive business case, you can download it (along with the summary version) at www.symbiapartners .com/mentalfitnessresources.

What I've done is look at the argument in a number of different ways:

- **What is the cost of doing nothing?** For example, what is the negative impact of acute stress, anxiety, burnout, and depression (mental illness) on business?
- **What's the benefit of doing something more?** For example, how does investing in mental wellness positively affect engagement, retention, and productivity?
- Finally, I look at **the further positive impact of investing in mental fitness** – strengthening and enhancing the mental and emotional well-being of our workforce to positively impact performance.

Mental Health: The Magnitude of the Problem

Poor mental health is a huge cost to businesses and the economy. According to The WHO, the world economy loses about US$1 trillion per year in productivity due to depression and anxiety. That's the equivalent of $130 per person on the planet!

Table 2.1 illustrates the magnitude of diagnosed mental health illness globally. The numbers are so huge that it may be difficult to imagine how this impacts your business. So, to bring it closer to home, imagine a global team of 30 people. Three of your colleagues may *currently* be suffering some mental health problems. This is likely to rise during the current COVID-19 pandemic. People at work in 2020 have faced unprecedented levels of disruption and change, not only with their own work but with their family situation.

Table 2.1   Global statistics on the scale of mental health illness.

Statistic	Source
One in four have suffered mental health illness at some point in their lives	The WHO[1]
One in two American adults are diagnosed with a mental illness at some point in their lives	CDC USA[2]
One in 10 (792 million) people are currently suffering mental health illness	IHME[3]

[1] World Health Organization (2019) 'Mental health', *World Health Organization* <https://www.who.int/news-room/facts-in-pictures/detail/mental-health>
[2] Centers for Disease Control and Prevention USA (2018) *Mental Health Data and Publications,* Centers for Disease Control and Prevention USA <https://www.cdc.gov/mentalhealth/data_publications/index.htm>
[3] IHME (Institute for Health Metrics and Evaluation) (2017) *Global Burden of Disease.*

The Tip of the Iceberg

If we overlook (or under-support) people with mental health issues, we risk overlooking a significant proportion of the working population. In the UK, people with mental health problems make up a significant proportion of the workforce. However, diagnosed mental health issues are only the tip of the iceberg. Mental health at work is not limited to just diagnosed conditions. We should consider mental health problems as any mental health problems that are *brought to, experienced at, or caused by work*. This is more common than you might think.

So, thinking of your team of 30 again, potentially 9 people have experienced mental health problems at some point, and 5 of them still are; and 18 members of your team have experienced stress or problems caused by their job at some point. When a member of your team is experiencing stress or anxiety at work, we should be striving to create an open environment where workers are able to get help within the workplace before they report sick. However, in an increasing number of cases, this just isn't happening (Table 2.2).

Now, look at your team and think about the potential you could unlock with a mental fitness programme. Not only could you support these people now, you would also enhance and strengthen their mental and emotional well-being for the future, not just for those people suffering now, but for all 30 of your figurative team. Isn't that something worth investigating? I think so.

The Cost of Doing Nothing (or Not Doing Enough)

The cost to business is huge. *The Lancet*[3a] estimates 12 billion days (equivalent to US$925 billion) worldwide in lost productivity are

---

[3a]WHO & The Lancet Psychiatry 2016: Scaling-up treatment of depression and anxiety: a global return on investment analysis

Table 2.2   UK statistics on the scale of mental health illness and work-related stress.

Statistic	Source	Impact on your team of 30		
People with mental health problems make up 15.9% of the UK workforce	Oxford Economics[4]	Five out of 30	Experiencing NOW	
One in four (23%) UK employees have experienced symptoms of mental health problems in the past month, related to or caused by work	BITC[5]	Eight out of 30		
30% of the UK workforce is diagnosed with a mental health condition in their lifetime		Nine out of 30	At some point	
Six in 10 (62%) UK employees have experienced symptoms of mental health problems, related to or caused by work, at some point in their career		18 out of 30		

attributable to depression and anxiety *every year*. That's the equivalent of taking the *entire* UK workforce out of production for a year.

The costs are due to four main factors: absenteeism, presenteeism, leaveism, and labour turnover (Figure 2.1).

---

[4]Oxford Economics Analysis, 'The economic importance of safeguarding mental health in the workplace,' *Mental Health Foundation* <https://www.mentalhealth.org.uk/publications/added-value-mental-health-workplace-asset>

[5]Business in the Community (2019) 'Mental health at work 2019: time to take ownership', BitC <https://www.bitc.org.uk/report/mental-health-at-work-2019-time-to-take-ownership/>

Absenteeism	**Presenteeism**	**Leaveism**	**Labour Turnover**
Where employees take time off due to ill health. The numbers recorded though are often under-estimated as people do not always disclose the real reason is due to mental health.	Where employees work, but are under-productive due to poor emotional wellbeing.	The growing tendency of the inability to 'switch off' from work is leading to more people leaving their jobs. As working remotely has become increasingly common, it can lead to overworking, reduction in workforce morale, and burnout.	The increased costs of training & recruitment, plus the costs of temporary staff to cover a role when vacant.

Figure 2.1   Factors affecting business performance.

A 2020 study by Deloitte in the UK[6] estimates that the costs to private sector business are up to £35.2 billion per year. This is made up of:

- £21.1–£23.4 billion in presenteeism
- £6.9 billion in turnover costs
- £5 billion in absence

The same study shows that the average employer is losing £1652 per employee due to poor mental health, and that the average ROI for well-being initiatives is 5×. Despite this excellent investment opportunity, the average UK employer is spending just £26 per employee per year, compared to £210 in Sweden.

---

[6]Deloitte UK (2020, January) *Mental Health and Employers: Refreshing the Case for Investment*, <https://www2.deloitte.com/uk/en/pages/consulting/articles/mental-health-and-employers-refreshing-the-case-for-investment.html>

Presenteeism and leaveism are increasingly prevalent in the workplace as communication advances mean we are unable to 'switch off' from work. Some eye-watering statistics are listed below:

- 73% of British workers feel they are expected to be available for work at all times.[7]

- 9% of workers in the UK who have no experience of mental health problems agree that 'distress has left them less productive than they would like'.[8]

- 51% of organisations observed that employees work outside contracted hours to get work done.[9]

- 36% observed employees would use holidays and other allocated time off to work.[11]

- In a global study, nearly one in three workers are 'unable to mentally switch off from work', and 20% of people said 'being constantly connected to work made them feel mentally exhausted'.[10]

- When asked the question, 'When I am struggling with my mental health and would benefit from time off', 85% of UK respondents agreed they would still 'always or mostly go to work'.[11]

Gallup's 'State of the Global Workplace 2016' measures employee engagement and well-being. Worldwide, two thirds of the workforce

---

[7] Unum (2014) *The Future Workplace*, Unum <http:/resources.unum.co.uk/downloads/future-workplace.pdf?cdbc2a5e-58fb-5feb-9dda-6058155b6f58>

[8] Mental Health Foundation (2016) *Added Value: Mental Health as a Workplace Asset*, https://www.mentalhealth.org.uk/publications/added-value-mental-health-workplace-asset

[9] CIPD (2020) *Health and Well-Being at Work*, CIPD

[10] The Myers-Briggs Company (2019) *Type and the Always-On Culture*, The Myers-Briggs Company <https://ap.themyersbriggs.com/content/Type_and_the_always_on_culture__TheMyersBriggsCo_2019.pdf>

[11] MIND (UK) (2018–2019) *Workplace Wellbeing Index*, <https://www.mind.org.uk/media-a/5990/mind-index-insight-report-2019.pdf>

are 'not engaged' in their jobs, and 18% are 'actively disengaged'.[12] The study also measures and reports on the well-being of populations, using five key essential elements: purpose, social, community, financial, and physical. The report found that in the United States, 28% of adults are 'struggling or suffering' in all of these elements, while only 19% are thriving in at least four out of the five.

Why is this important in the workplace? Well, even engaged employees are more likely to miss work days, are slower to recover from illness, and are more likely to be looking for another job if their well-being is poor. Imagine having a workforce with purpose, with good work relationships, feeling part of a community. That's what consciously and positively investing in a well-being (and better still, mental fitness) programme can bring to your business. Engaged, thriving employees who are less likely to take time off, and are more productive at work, more resilient and happy to embrace change.

Enough of the costs of doing *nothing*. Let's look at the benefits of doing something.

The Benefits of Taking Action: The Bottom Line

Benefits to the Economy

People with mental health challenges should not be written off, as they deliver significantly more benefits than costs for the global economy. People with mental health problems – working in a wide range of industries, from construction to entertainment – made an estimated £226 billion gross-value-added contribution to UK GDP in 2015. To put this into perspective, without them, the economy would shrink by 12.1%.[13]

---

[12] GALLUP-Healthways (2015) *Well-Being Index*.
[13] Mental Health Foundation (2016) *Added Value: Mental Health as a Workplace Asset* <https://www.mentalhealth.org.uk/publications/added-value-mental-health-workplace-asset>

Businesses with developed well-being programmes have shown that it is possible to reduce the costs associated with staff mental health problems. If just 10% of the costs were mitigated, Oxford Economics calculate the UK economy could be £3.3 billion larger than it otherwise would be in 2030 (0.1% of forecasted GDP that year).[14]

Benefits to Business

Despite all the evidence showing the costs to employers and the economy of poor mental health in the workplace, barriers to investment in workplace mental health remain, including a lack of evidence that such investments can have a positive impact on the bottom line.

However, employers who do embark on well-being programmes believe there will be benefits to investing in this way. According to a global survey by XEROX in 2016,[15] increasing employee productivity (59%) is now the top objective of a well-being programme, followed closely by improving employee engagement and morale (56%).

Thriving employees not only cost their employers less, they are more productive and more engaged in their work.

According to US research by The Healthways Center of Health Research,[16] as well-being increases, direct and indirect costs decrease, and employee performance improves. *A 10% increase in well-being was associated with 24% lower presenteeism and 6% more 'best work' days per month.*

Studies around the world have started to yield real-world evidence that workplace programmes focusing on enhancing the mental and

---

[14] Oxford Economics analysis, *The Economic Importance of Safeguarding Mental Health in the Workplace,* Mental Health Foundation, <https://www.mentalhealth.org.uk/publications/added-value-mental-health-workplace-asset>

[15] XEROX (2016) *Working Well: A Global Survey of Workforce Wellbeing Strategies,* XEROX <https://www.xerox.com/downloads/usa/en/buck/reports/hrc_rp_global_wellbeing_survey_2016.pdf>

[16] The Healthways Center of Health Research and Population Health Management (2012)

Table 2.3   Return on investment: mental health and well-being programmes.

Source	Detail	ROI
Deloitte UK[17]	Mental Health and Employers ROI analysis (2019)	5:1
Deloitte USA & Canada[18]	The ROI in work health programs (2018)	2.68:1
PWC Australia[19]	Creating a mentally healthy workplace return on investment analysis (2014)	Between 2.3:1 and 14:1

emotional well-being of employees are an investment that yields valuable returns, rather than a cost (Table 2.3).

The Benefits of Taking Action: A Mentally Fit Workforce

The ROIs in the studies referenced above look at the quantifiable returns of employee wellness programmes in terms of reductions in absenteeism, increased productivity, and reduced turnover. But what of the other benefits? How can we quantify the benefits to an organisation willing to invest beyond the absence of illness and strive for enhancing the mental fitness of their employees? A study conducted for The World Economic Forum[20] highlights this perfectly.

---

[17] Deloitte UK (2020, January) *Mental Health and Employers: Refreshing the Case for Investment.*
[18] Deloitte USA and Canada (2018) *The ROI in Work Health Programs: Good for People, Good for Business: A Blueprint for Workplace Mental Health Programs.*
[19] PWC Australia (2014) *Creating a Mentally Healthy Workplace: Return on Investment Analysis.*
[20] The World Economic Forum (2010) *The Wellness Imperative – Creating More Effective Organizations,* WEF

Their survey spoke to employees across multiple organisations and asked their view on how their company performs. According to employees in organisations where health and well-being are actively promoted:

- Organisations are seen as 2.5 times more likely to be a best performer (in their field).

- Organisations are seen as 3 times more likely to be productive.

- Organisations are seen as 3.5 times more likely to encourage creativity and innovation.

- Organisations are seen as 4 times less likely to lose talent within the next year.

- Employees are 8 times more likely to be engaged.

So, the takeaway from this is that thriving employees (those who have benefited from such programmes) are *eight times more likely to be engaged employees*. Engaged employees bring multiple benefits to organisations. In the United States, a Gallup survey[21] highlights the positive metrics associated with being engaged and thriving at work (Figure 2.2).

For instance, take the metric adaptability and think about how this might benefit a company embarking on a restructure. An alarming statistic from research conducted by McKinsey[22] shows that there's a *70% rate of failure in business transformations*. One of the key reasons stated by McKinsey is, 'People throughout the organization don't buy in, and they don't want to invest extra energy to make change happen.' One factor that is frequently undervalued and dismissed is mindset,

---

[21] Sorenson, S. (2013) *How Employee Engagement Drives Growth*, GALLUP <https://www.gallup.com/workplace/236927/employee-engagement-drives-growth.aspx>
[22] McKinsey (2015) *Changing Change Management*, McKinsey <https://www.mckinsey.com/featured-insights/leadership/changing-change-management>

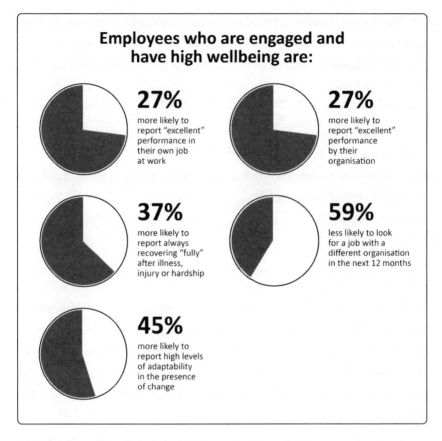

Figure 2.2 Benefits to having engaged employees.

but we also know that mindset is the most important driver of exceptional strategic execution:

- In organisations identified as extremely successful, 72% of respondents noted that the transformation 'entirely' or 'very much' took mindset into account.

- In those organisations identified as not at all successful, this number drops to 8%.

We know from numerous studies that emotional intelligence leads to a better ability to manage our emotions and thoughts, and this ability leads to better mental health outcomes (less stress, anxiety, negative thinking), which both directly and indirectly lead to better performance over time.

In a case study on Unilever (found at the end of this book), where a programme of mental fitness had been undertaken, it was reported that employees embraced the change so successfully that *77% of participants claimed an increase in performance and increased their overall motivation by 15%.*

In the UK, the 2020 CIPD *Health and Well-Being at Work* study[23] analysed the impact of well-being initiatives in the private sector. This study found 58% of organisations had better employee morale and engagement, 49% a healthier and more inclusive atmosphere, and 29% reduced work-related stress; while 16% reported better customer service, showing that well-being initiatives really permeate all parts of the organisation.

All these benefits ultimately lead to benefits to shareholders too. According to Deloitte USA,[24] companies in the S&P 500 with high health and wellness scores had a stock appreciation of 235% compared to 159% overall.

Through this chapter, we have put forward the huge costs of mental health in the workplace, to the world, and national economies. We have also put forward that for every $1 spent on wellness programmes in business, returns on that investment are calculated to be anywhere from $2–$14. We have also written about mental fitness,

[23]CIPD (2020) *Health and Well-Being at Work,* CIPD <https://www.cipd.co.uk/Images/private-sector-summary_tcm18-73786.pdf>
[24]Deloitte USA and Canada (2018) *The ROI in Work Health Programs: Good for People, Good for Business: A Blueprint for Workplace Mental Health Programs.*

and how having employees who don't merely exist but ***thrive*** in the workplace will help your organisation transform, will help its creativity and its innovation.

Mental fitness isn't just about reducing the costs associated with mental illness; it's about enabling people to access all of their inner resources – equipping people to make the most of their talents and skills.

Mental fitness really matters for the future. More now, post COVID, than ever. We need our employees to be agile, resilient, and able to cope with what the new normal throws at them. The organisations that are more likely to succeed in this new environment are those with good, authentic wellness programmes – and those programmes will have to include elements of mental fitness. We've shown in this chapter that a company with a good wellness programme will have employees who are engaged and feel looked after. In return, the employees care about the company they work for, their boss, and they want to keep going because they feel 'we're in this together'.

We face a turbulent future. We face a future where companies will have to re-evaluate the skills their employees need to survive in what's going to be a very tough market over the next few years. A mentally and emotionally fit workforce will be essential to succeed.

If you would like to have the in-depth version of this business case, it can be downloaded from www.symbiapartners.com/mentalfitnessresources.

This belief that we have inner resources that can give us an edge, that's a great and exciting thing … Accessing the inner resources of a human being. This is a source of competitive advantage.

– Tim Munden, Chief Learning Officer, Unilever

Mental fitness really matters for the future. We need agile and resilient leaders to secure our future. So, we have to make people understand that you've got to train your muscles, your mental muscles, to become more resilient and more agile for the future because the pace of change is rapidly increasing and we are constantly expecting more from each other in less time, therefore this is a vital skill to master. This isn't something you do because you're feeling a bit of stress, actually it's much more than that. It's about making yourself ready to become the type of leader we need for the future. It's really important that this is positioned as it should be – it's about developing our leaders to be mentally and emotionally fit for the future they must lead us into – one where we need to be adaptable and agile in the face of constant change.

– Nathalie Slechte, Chief HR Officer, JDE

3 The Future of Fit Businesses

At 3:40 pm Sam leans back in his chair and stretches. He finishes up with what he's working on and then stands and walks to the kitchen to get a glass of water. On the way, he pauses by Jenny's desk. Sam smiles at her as she glances up from her screen and sees him standing there. 'How are you getting on with your project? Did you find a solution to the supply chain hold-up?' he asks.

Jenny smiles back, 'Actually yes, that one-to-one we had yesterday really helped. After I was able to 'get out of the weeds' and we'd looked at the big picture together, I had another idea about how we could make this work so I'm putting together a plan this afternoon.'

'Great! I'd love to hear more about this, but let's chat later, I'm just on my way to a meeting.' Sam flashes another smile and Jenny nods. He heads for the kitchen and checks his watch: 3:45 pm. Taking a sip of the cool water in his glass, he pauses. The meeting he's on his way to is his six-monthly performance review.

Sam isn't nervous; in fact, he's feeling good about the meeting. These reviews used to be daunting, but he's reframed his thinking and now sees that they present an opportunity to learn and improve, whether the feedback he receives is positive or negative. Before he goes in though, he knows the importance of taking a moment to centre himself before he steps into the conference room so that he is calm and can give himself time to reflect on what's said, rather than reacting and potentially becoming defensive or frustrated.

He arrives at the door a minute later, glass of water in one hand and a pen and pad of paper in the other. He knocks gently, knowing that his boss will already be there. 'Come in.' Sam pushes the door open and sees Peter, already settled on one side of the table. Peter smiles. 'Sam, early as usual. Come in and get comfortable. Jo will join us in a moment.'

Sam returns the smile, nods, and takes his seat across from Peter. They're enjoying a conversation about how they each spent their weekends when Jo enters the room. Realising that she's the last to arrive, she checks her watch. Sam smiles at her, 'Don't worry Jo, you're not late. Peter and I are both just very early.'

She laughs. 'Of course you both are!' After a few more minutes of chatting about family and the weather, they begin to run through Sam's review.

Peter takes the lead. 'Sam, I think it's safe to say that we've all been impressed with how you've taken on the leadership of your team in the past year. You've been the steady hand they really needed, and we've seen a noticeable improvement in the performance of the team since you took it on.'

Sam nods. 'Thank you. My team have worked very hard in the past six months, and we're still working on improving the decision-making process, but I feel as though we've made good progress.'

Jo jumps in. 'We can see from the figures that you've made progress in a number of areas, Sam. It's clear that you're helping everyone to make much more considered and strategic decisions. Having sat in on a few of your meetings, I've seen the way in which you encourage open-mindedness and positivity in your team and how you get them to step back and consider alternative viewpoints and opportunities, as well as consider challenges they might have missed. They needed someone with a steady hand and that strategic oversight.'

As the meeting progresses, they dive into details and figures. Sam takes notes about what is working within his team and where there is room for improvement. As the hour comes to an end, he feels satisfied with the outcome and ready to move forward with his team.

Sam's positive performance review didn't happen by accident. It's no coincidence that his team is performing well and that he's considered to be a steady, wise, and calm leader. Sam invests in his mental fitness, and that of his teams; this is what makes the difference, both to him and his team. Let's take a look at how he does that.

When Sam goes to bed, he sets his alarm 15 minutes earlier than he needs to wake up because he wants to have time to reflect. The first half hour of his morning is taken up with this gradual waking and reflection, followed by a meditation practice. With the first rays of sunlight breaking over the horizon, Sam pulls on his running kit and steps outside. The air is fresh and still. He pauses, taking in the sounds, smells, and sights around him before he sets off on a jog. This half-hour run is one part of his routine that he's careful to never skip, because he knows the exercise sets him up for the day.

By the time he returns, his son and daughter are up and in the kitchen with his wife. He greets them all warmly as he makes his morning smoothie that always follows his run, full of fresh fruit and vegetables (and sometimes a dollop of peanut butter as a treat).

Sam loves having breakfast with his family in the morning. It reminds him of what's important, and even when his daughter is refusing to eat her toast because it still has the crusts on, he has to smile. He knows it's about picking your battles, so he removes the crusts and encourages her to eat.

As he leaves to get the train into work, he tells his family he loves them. The half-hour train journey is another chance for him to calm his mind. He doesn't check his emails or even think about work; instead he loses himself in a good book. Just like his morning run, this too is a source of energy for him.

When Sam arrives in the office, he goes to his desk and turns on his computer, but he doesn't sit down immediately. He goes to the kitchen and on the way makes a point of saying good morning to everyone who's already in the office. He chats as he makes his coffee, and he's not in a rush to get back to his desk.

Every Monday, Sam starts his day by deciding what his three areas of focus for the week should be. These are his three big 'rocks', and once he has those, he'll map out potential distractions and find ways to avoid them, such as turning off his email notifications, or blocking windows of time in his day so they don't get stolen by unexpected meeting invites.

At 10.30 am on Mondays, he has a regular meeting with his team. The first 10 minutes is always reserved for general chat. He likes to know how they are, how they spent their weekends, and how they're feeling as they start the week. Each person shares their own three focus areas for the week, so that the rest of the team is aware of what's going on.

Sam isn't afraid to say no to meetings or interruptions that don't relate to his three focus areas. Is it hard? Yes, but he does it anyway as he knows he needs to protect his time. Unless it's something truly urgent, he skilfully avoids those additional meetings that often sneak into his diary.

His lunch break is sacred, and he always makes sure that he leaves the building for half an hour to get a proper break from the office. Sam also knows that staring at a screen rarely solves problems, so he will happily take a break to chat to a member of his team, or even to pop to the floor above and check in with the marketing team or HR.

That's not to say Sam doesn't get stressed; of course he does. Like all of us, he has moments where he can feel his emotions rising and his heart rate spiking, but he's aware of this and has been consciously working on it. He makes sure to negotiate some time to solve problems to ensure he's not making hasty decisions or sending emotionally driven emails.

One of his skills, which he is also fostering in his team, is his ability to take himself out of a situation and view the bigger picture. This allows him to consider whether what he's about to say or do could be harmful for himself, someone else, or the business; and it means he's able to find the solution that will lead to the right end goal. Sam knows that the easy choices aren't always the right choices. It's a lesson he's trying to teach his team.

He makes a point of leaving the office no later than 6 pm each day. There will always be more work to do, and that work will still be there when he turns up tomorrow. He knows if he doesn't set his limits no one else will. He dives back into his book on his train ride home, leaving whatever has happened in his business day at the office so that he's fresh for his family when he gets home.

All of these small habits that Sam has developed enable him to show up to work each day with the energy to perform at a high level and the ability to be strategic and calm. Sam considers his inner resources – his mind and his emotions – to be a priority. He knows the importance of switching off and disconnecting in order to rejuvenate, replenish, and restore.

What would it look like if all the employees and leaders in your organisation showed up every day with this attitude, self-awareness, focus, and composure? What could the impact be on the company as a whole? How much more engaged and focused might people be? How would that impact the bottom line?

This is the future of fit businesses. Historically we've seen businesses trying to incentivise people with external influences like salaries, bonuses, and benefits that are all linked to the business. Developing a fit business for the future requires organisations to understand that there is an untapped and largely unrecognised resource within all of us.

If you can tap into the inner energy that each of your employees has, this will enable them to perform at their best, which can positively impact their experience of the world along with influencing the bottom line. In the previous chapter, I shared with you the business cost of doing nothing to tackle mental and emotional challenges, such as stress, depression, and anxiety. There is a human cost as well as a business cost associated with this.

When you move towards the concept of mental fitness, it's no longer about the cost of doing nothing but about the benefits of doing something. These benefits are emotional, behavioural, financial, and performance related. There are benefits to the individual, business, and society as a whole if we are willing to invest in enhancing the mental fitness of our workforce.

What I'm asking you to do now is to move away from this idea of mental health and well-being, and even performance in general, and just consider what's required to operate in an accelerated world. Because the rate of change is continuously accelerating, what we need more than ever is a more adaptable and agile workforce. We need people who have inner resources that they can tap into in order to help navigate change and adapt to challenges and setbacks.

The business landscape is already becoming more agile and nimble, with more start-ups and small brands appearing in local markets. Big companies don't have the nimbleness and agility to respond to them, not only because of process and structure, but also because their people aren't used to the rapid pace and mental agility that's required to respond. Even an adaptable business model and agile structure is worthless if the people who implement them don't have agile mindsets and behaviours.

Having a workforce that has the ability to be agile, adapt to change, and think creatively to solve problems and challenges is a strong competitive advantage for the future. Developing this kind of workforce isn't only important for businesses, but it's also important for us as people. With the skills that I'm going to share in the rest of this book, you will be able to improve the quality of your life as well as the performance of your business.

The key to the mental fitness movement is that we're not relying on other people to solve our problems, because by having greater self-awareness, self-regulation skills, and an understanding of our minds, emotions, thoughts, and behaviours, we become empowered.

Many leaders face constant tension between the needs of the business and the needs of their people. By helping your people become empowered and more autonomous, you give yourself more freedom because you will no longer have to be a coach, therapist, and business mentor as well as a leader. When your team learn to access their own inner resources, they will require less of yours.

The beauty of what we're doing is making everybody responsible for their own performance, energy, and well-being. We're encouraging people to understand why they do what they do, why and how they are showing up in business, how they plan to contribute, and how they can have a positive impact in everything they do. This comes back to the concepts of self-awareness, self-regulation, empathy, and relationship management, all of which are the 'hidden edge' of life and of business.

In helping your employees to be more accountable and responsible within their own lives, each person becomes better equipped to support themselves and others within their team. They have the energy to perform and to show up not only for their teams, but also for their families and for the overall business.

A secondary benefit to this is that it frees you up as a leader to focus on what you're really there to do, which is inspire, lead, and make the right decisions for the business. When you are confident in the knowledge that your people are anchored and grounded, and that they have perspective, awareness, and wisdom, you can focus on your performance as a leader. This all leads to a fit organisation that is braver in its decision making, more resilient in the face of setbacks, and more agile in an ever-changing marketplace.

I would definitely suggest any business that isn't currently focusing on employee wellbeing and mental fitness should think about what the component parts of the high-performing organisation are and what this means for them in terms of the skills their employees need to have to succeed in what's going to be a very tough market over the next three to five years. The pressures of digitisation will come together and I think some pretty relentless economic pressures will be felt by organisations. So, how are they going to support the people with the right capabilities to thrive in that sort of very challenging and uncertain environment? I would suggest they remember that people having resilience, positivity and mental fitness is a core capability.

— Head of Wellbeing, Global Financial Services

The fact that it [mental fitness work] impacts the business and impacts your life makes it the dream thing to invest in. If I think about the business case and return on investment, the return on investment is huge because the real investment is people's time. Because they believe in it and are going to be thinking about it afterwards, it's almost infinite in the sense that it affects so many things. What it takes from us [as a business] is to get the ball rolling and to keep pulsing with additional help, challenges, growth and development.

— Shawn Conway, CEO, Peet's Coffee

Part Two
The Power of Meaning and Emotions

Now that you understand why mental fitness matters, and can see the business case underlying it, we didn't want to leave you scratching your heads as to how you can enhance yours. The rest of the book is dedicated to equipping you with the knowledge and tools that you need to improve your own mental fitness, and hopefully the mental fitness of your teams (as it's your duty to pass the knowledge on).

It's important to acknowledge the emotional, cognitive, and behavioural worlds that we as humans have within us. Meaning penetrates all of these worlds and ties them together. We're going to begin our journey by delving into the emotional world, because this is often the element that we are least sure of and know least about navigating.

More specifically, I'm going to start by exploring perception, because it is the gateway between our inner and outer worlds.

The most important knowledge I want to impart to you is that perception is interpretive. We overlay meaning onto what we see, and what we believe is reality, is actually interpretation.

Acknowledging that we overlay meaning onto topics, and understanding the effect this has on our emotional and cognitive states, as well as on our decision making and ultimately our actions, is the foundation of mental fitness.

Imagine having a team that had an enhanced awareness and were able to self-regulate when charged with stress, uncertainty, or challenge. How would that impact their performance?

4 Perception: Do You See What I See?

Have you ever heard the term 'meta-thinking'? Meta-thinking is the ability to think about our thinking. It's one of the aspects that distinguishes humans from the rest of the animal kingdom: the ability to self-reflect and look at oneself from afar. But how often do we do it? Perhaps when we are daydreaming, imagining a future scenario, or reliving a past event.

Not just this; how many of us have dug deep enough to truly know what 'makes us tick'? What are our typical thinking patterns? Our habitual emotional responses? Our core values and beliefs? Most of us have some ideas around these questions, and if we've experienced any type of therapy we might have more insight.

Why this topic is not taught in schools will always mystify me.

Why do we have to wait until we find ourselves in therapy before learning these 'secrets'? Wouldn't life be easier if we learned a bit more about how our minds and emotions work? How might it improve our lives if we practised emotional regulation and could understand how to live with emotion rather than be swept away by it?

It's our thinking and emotions that are ultimately influencing our decisions in life; and the outcomes of our decisions give us our life's experience. But many tend to let it all happen subconsciously and unpoliced. We have 1,000-page manuals for our washing machines, but none for our minds. Well, it's time that changed. Where better place to start than the topic of thinking, and, more specifically, perception.

Perception is the gateway between our external world and our internal world.

It's what we *observe* to be happening, or more accurately it's how we *interpret* what is happening, which helps give meaning to the world around us. Our perception is fed via all our senses in the moment, but it is also coloured by past events.

As life passes us by so quickly, it's rare that we stop to examine our perception. More often than not we are 'subject' to it, rather than seeing it for what it often is, 'one interpretation' of events.

> We don't see things as they are, we see things as we are.
>
> – *Anais Nin*

I'm sure many of you have seen the following illusion (Figure 4.1) before, which is why I'm using it. Tell me, what do you see?

Some of you will see an old woman, some of you a young woman, some of you both. If you can only see the young woman, try now to see the old woman. If you only see the old woman, try and change your perception to see the young woman.

It's difficult, isn't it? Here is a hint – if you're trying to see the young woman, then consider the 'wart' or bump on the old woman to actually be the small side-angled nose of the young woman. The young woman's ear is the old woman's eye. If you can only see the old woman, do the opposite. Consider her mouth to actually be a necklace/choker.

The issue is, when you can only see one you get fixated, and it can be a real challenge to open your mind to see the alternatives.

Figure 4.1 Young woman/old woman.

Source: © Science History Images / Alamy Stock Photo

I've shown this image to thousands of people around the world from all walks of life. In executive workshops, I'll always get two people to stand up (one who can only see the old woman but not the young woman, and then the reverse). I then give them the job of helping the other person see what they see. Sometimes it takes 5 minutes, sometimes 20 minutes, and sometimes they just CANNOT help the other person see it (without cheating and highlighting it in a different colour for them).

It always leads to a lot of laughter, but the insight is not lost on anyone. Even when we point something out to someone on a big screen, it can still be hard to change their perception.

Let's try another one.

When you look at this picture (Figure 4.2), what do you notice? Does anything stand out to you?

Figure 4.2   What do you see?[1]

How about now (see Figure 4.3)?

I've had rooms of people shout out 'peacock!', 'lady lying down in a meadow!', 'a bird swooping to the ground' – all sorts of answers.

But can you see the cow? It's rare that people see the cow until it's pointed out. Then you can't *not* see the cow.

How we see the world is not always how it is.

It's extremely difficult to demonstrate that in other ways, but perceptual illusions make it possible to point directly at the different ways something can be seen. Let me explain further.

We (and our brains) experience the outside world through our senses. It's common knowledge that we have five senses, but indeed we actually have many more. We have a sense of balance, pain, temperature, and so on. We use all this information, both from the past (memories) and the present, to interpret the world around us.

All this data is sent to the brain, where it is used to formulate ideas and opinions, to interpret events or situations, to create reactions and responses. All this information influences us, because our

[1]John McCrone 1990, *"The Ape that spoke – Language and the evolution of the human mind"*, Macmillan, Public Domain-CC-by-3.0, Retrieved from <*https://commons.wikimedia.org/wiki/File:Cow_Illusion.jpg*>

Figure 4.3 Can you see the cow?[2]

experience of the world, past events, and memories all shape our future interpretations.

Not only do they shape our interpretations but also our expectations. Collectively, the information influences our thoughts, our emotions, our beliefs – and therefore our behaviours. If you can anchor your thinking, you can consciously choose your behaviour. Applying this level of thinking to organisations at every level is powerful; it drives some incredible results. To really harness it though, let's dig a little deeper.

The Science of Vision

Neuroscientists tell us that one third of the brain's cortex is engaged in vision; it is the most prioritised sense. But that doesn't mean we see exactly what's there – we still make mistakes. There is a tendency to think of vision as a camera, but we often 'snap' *more* than what is transmitted by the optic nerve to the brain; we 'snap' more of a picture than we end up actually seeing.

---

[2]John McCrone 1990, *"The Ape that spoke – Language and the evolution of the human mind"*, Macmillan, Public Domain-CC-by-3.0, Retrieved from <*https://commons.wikimedia.org/wiki/File: Cow_Illusion.jpg*>

Millions of neurons and synapses are engaged in vision. They work hard to interpret what we see, so much so they often fill in the 'gaps' for us, gaps we didn't even know were there. In other words, the brain forms hypotheses, which work so well we often don't question them.

> Understanding vision and the most basic things about what the brain holds is the secret to understanding what it is to be human. Not just what we see but how and why we see it.
> – *Beau Lotto, a leading neuroscientist and expert in perception*

As Beau Lotto points out, 'Our brains CONSTRUCT what we need to see in the moment and see the world the way it is useful to see it, not necessarily the way it IS. We make these leaps of faith, fill in the gaps, take artistic licence, project our own feelings, emotions and experiences on to things ... all to help ourselves make sense of what's going on'.[3]

To explore this theory, my team and I ran a small social experiment and asked people to describe the emotion on this guy's face (Figure 4.4).

Figure 4.4   What's the emotion?

---

[3]TED (2009, July) *Beau Lotto: Optical illusions show how we see* [Video] <https://www.ted.com/talks/beau_lotto_optical_illusions_show_how_we_see?language=en>

You'd think it would be quite straightforward. But as you can see from this word map (Figure 4.5), we had a myriad of different descriptions, so many different words to describe the emotion, from confused, anxious, ashamed to stuck and surprised; they're on a complete spectrum. But we were all looking at the same face.

We ran this experiment not only to test the theory that we interpret things in different ways, but importantly to see if this theory extends itself to how we interpret emotions. You can see that the answer is yes. What does this tell us? We're learning that perception is subjective, not objective.

We filter things through our mind's eye. Why is this important? It's important because *who* we are is influencing what we see. Our moods, our beliefs, our experiences all have a role to play. If you were in a bad mood when you answered the question 'What's the facial expression on this man's face?', you were more likely to say, 'He's in a bad mood. He's annoyed. He's angry'. That is because we project our emotions. Who we are and how we're feeling at any given moment is colouring our interpretation of the world. So, just as perceptual illusions exist, so, too, do other cognitive illusions. We can *think* one thing and take it for fact, without challenging it or without seeking out alternative viewpoints.

Let's imagine someone says something or does something in a meeting, and maybe you are upset or angry about it. You have seen

Figure 4.5 Emotion word map.

it one way, so perhaps you decide to do something like send an email, or make a decision in a slightly different way *because* of it.

The challenge is, you don't have someone walking out of the room after you, tapping you on the shoulder and pointing at a screen to say, 'Look, you saw it this way, but what you didn't see was this ...' Because all of this happens in your head and it happens in an instant. Other people often don't know how we are interpreting things; it happens so quickly, often *we* don't even know.

So, we need to be that person. We need to be the one who knows not to take everything at face value, the person who is willing to not react in the moment, but pause, reflect, and consider what other influences are at play. Dr Marc Brackett calls this 'being emotional scientists'.

What we tell ourselves about what we see or what we experience shapes our decisions in life, and the most important part about this is that we're not always right. If we have decided a member of our team at work is 'difficult', the only evidence we will see is the evidence that supports this. If we tell ourselves this project will never work, or gaining market share is impossible, that's the data we will pay most attention to.

This is called 'confirmation bias'. Our brain doesn't like contradictory information; it prefers to focus on information that supports our current thinking, so it can remain efficient. That's why it's so important to teach ourselves how to pause and how to see things from more than one angle before we take action.

If perception is never objective, but instead subjective, it's fundamentally important to be aware of our moods, beliefs, physiology, values, and experiences, because they are colouring our interpretation of the world – whether we are tuned into them or not.

So, if we're willing to change our perception, we can change our experience of the world, which of course impacts how we show up in life and in business. How do we do that? We need to know what makes us tick. We need to know who we are, what our thinking patterns are, what our default mindsets are, how we typically emotionally respond to situations. What are the experiences that are echoing in our lives today, and how are they colouring our perception?

I'd like you to consider for a moment three people in your team: your top performer, your average performer, and your lowest-performing team member. Write their names at the top of the column, and, below, I want you to write as many adjectives to describe them as possible.

Top performer	Average performer	Lowest performer

Now I want you to imagine you've been told that your lowest performer didn't have a great start in life. Their parents didn't nurture them academically; they were told by teachers that they'd never make it to university. They showed determination and grit and graduated through their own hard work even though it didn't come naturally to them, and they had no support from any adults in their life. Their families have generally worked in manual labour, the trades, or 'blue collar' jobs. They are the first in their family to have an office-based job. After they leave work every evening, they double-check all of their work and panic about not being like their other colleagues. They have deep-seated fears of not being good enough, but they struggle on, determined to work as hard as they can to prove that they deserve to be there.

Now I want you to revisit the column and choose new adjectives for your lowest performer.

Top performer	Average performer	Lowest performer

You see, we will win any game we're playing. If we've told ourselves a story about how or why someone isn't contributing or performing in the way we want, we will just see their failings. We will have a self-fulfilling prophecy. But what if there is more to their story than we realise? And even if there isn't, what if we just assume that every-one is trying their best, whatever context that's in? How would that change your leadership style? Might you be more willing to offer mentoring? Take extra time to coach? Invest in them slightly differently or encourage them a bit more? What would happen?

Well, you might just have a positive self-fulfilling prophecy on your hands instead. We can't change people, but we can change our attitudes to people. If we're aware of how the subtle biases in our minds are reinforcing our perhaps negative attitudes towards people, just that can be enough to change how we lead, nurture, and encourage the talent within our teams. Sometimes we are unwittingly contributing to predetermined outcomes. Stepping back and seeing that and then adjusting for it can be a game changer both for you as a leader and for your team.

Changing Perception: The Ladder of Inference

We've established that it's important to be aware of how we are interpreting the world around us. Not just what we're seeing but what we're telling ourselves about what we are seeing, because ultimately this is dictating our decisions in life AND we're not always getting it right. But KNOWING this isn't enough. Now it's time for real-life practice. On the next page, a simple tool to help apply this thinking to your life. It's called the Ladder of Inference (Figure 4.6), or, as I like to call it, the Ladder of Make-Believe. The model was first developed by Chris Argyris, building on the work of S.I. Hayakawa and Alford Korzybski, and articulated further by William Isaacs and Rick Ross.

We call it a ladder because throughout life and, in particular, in the workplace we tend to think of progress as climbing up ('the career ladder') and experiencing a new rung, or step, the higher we go. In this exercise, the steps of the ladder represent layers of thinking. It all starts with an event or situation that happens in your life. You observe it, and then you decide it means something. From that meaning you add assumptions, you then arrive at a conclusion which makes you believe something, and then you act. This happens instantaneously; you don't even realise all of these layers are being created and applied to your everyday reality.

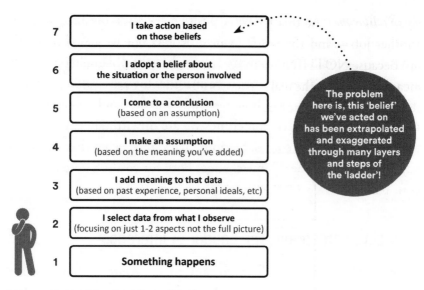

Figure 4.6   The Ladder of Inference.

Maybe you've spent the weekend working on a document. On Sunday night you send the work in an email to your boss. That's what happened, right? You observe that your boss doesn't respond to the email. You begin to overthink, your insecurities might creep in, overlaying meaning where there is none. You've worked hard all weekend and heard nothing. You decide that this maybe means she doesn't agree with your point of view on the topic. Maybe she doesn't really value your opinion. As time goes by and you think about it more, you might start to think *'she doesn't value ME, because she always takes a long time to reply'*.

As you ruminate on the lack of response, your thinking gets more exaggerated. You might begin to conclude that your boss doesn't like you, which makes you then believe, *'Well she never really liked me and maybe she never really liked the work I did anyway'*. As a result, you start to think and act differently towards her, you become strange and cautious, you become nervous about the work that you do and perhaps overcompensate in different ways. Then SHE starts to act a bit strangely around you and you think, *'Oh my, that's because my boss doesn't like me'.* At this point you start overthinking about getting another job – and the worst of it all is that you've just made it all up! Because NOTHING actually happened. You overlaid all the other meaning. What if the real reason your boss didn't respond was because she was in three days of training! (Figure 4.7)

What happened was...

I SENT IMPORTANT EMAIL TO MY BOSS

I observe that...

MY BOSS DIDN'T RESPOND

So, I decided this meant...

IT'S BECAUSE THEY DIDN'T
AGREE WITH MY OPINION

Because of this I assume...

THEY ALWAYS TAKE A LONG TIME
TO RESPOND TO ME, I THINK
THEY JUST DON'T VALUE ME

I then conclude...

THE ISSUE IS WITH ME...
THEY DON'T VALUE MY WORK...
THEY DON'T EVEN LIKE ME...

Which made me believe...

I THINK THEY THINK
I'M NOT THAT GOOD AT MY JOB

And so I...

ACT STRANGELY AROUND THEM...
START DOUBTING MY WORK...
START LOOKING FOR A NEW JOB!

Figure 4.7 Example of the ladder of inference.

We've used this example in our workshops, and we deliberately exaggerate it to make it fun, but the truth is pretty much EVERYONE can relate. We often get comments 'that was ME, just yesterday!'

Now, sometimes there is other information that you are being given that may validate some of your feelings. But usually these can be explained. The truth is, we don't reflect on our thinking often enough. Although our 'conclusions' might sometimes be right, often we are wrong, because we take more out of a situation and overlay more onto it than there is in the first place. We create meaning where meaning doesn't necessarily exist.

It's critically important to pay attention to the stories we tell ourselves. Especially when those stories get exaggerated in our heads so quickly and can end up affecting our behaviour. Shooting up the ladder is fine; it happens to us all, and sometimes we do it as a collective (group thinking). However, we need to be aware that we've done it and, more importantly, we need to have a way of climbing back down this ladder, just to double-check with ourselves that we're getting it right before we do anything crazy like quitting our job.

I have a simple technique you can use to climb back down that ladder.

Let's take that example that we've been using and put into our template on the next page (Figure 4.8).

Something happened: you sent an email to your boss. Then you climbed up the Ladder of Make-Believe. Once you're at the top of the ladder, it's important to challenge your thinking. Here is the tool that will enable you to think about it differently.

- My boss didn't reply. **But what I didn't see was** … *My boss was in three days of training.*

Three days of training: that's kind of important information that maybe you deleted or weren't fully aware of at the time.

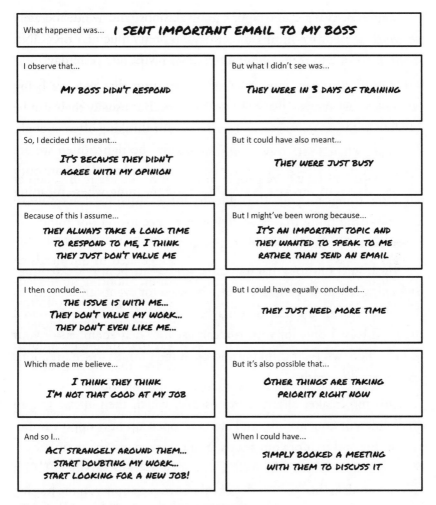

Figure 4.8 How we climb the ladder.

- She didn't agree with my opinion that was in the email. **But it could have also meant** . . . . *She was busy.*

Read through the exercise, and you can see how each prompt encourages you to open your perception and see things differently. It's a tool to help you see things that perhaps you wouldn't have seen before.

Sometimes we get so wrapped up in the story in our heads – what we *think* something means and therefore what that person thinks about us (trying to think about what other people are thinking is like trying to mind-read!) – that we forget to stop and challenge that very thinking. That maybe, just maybe, there's a way we can see it from a different angle.

That's when THIS tool is most useful.

Perhaps you may have people in your life who are really good at reframing things for you. The difficulty is that often we don't want to talk about the thing that is worrying us or occupying our minds, in which case you should use this template.

The beauty of this is that it doesn't just have to be applied to things happening in our present; it can also be used for events and situations that happened in the past that maybe you still feel bad or frustrated about. This isn't only for you. You can use it to help members of your team break down their thinking and open their minds to see situations and events differently.

This tool makes alternatives possible, which then allows you to draw different conclusions, and starts to open up new opportunities in your life and that of your teams. You can even use the template for creative brainstorming. We have a tendency to fixate on one solution for one problem, but the Ladder of Inference can show you the hidden assumptions made along the way and open your and your team's eyes to other potential areas for exploration. Some people don't even need to use the tool; just knowing that there is such a thing called 'The ladder of inference' introduces new language into their lives. New language means we can 'label' things. Sometimes it's enough to say 'Wow, I just shot up the ladder of inference' and that can be enough to interrupt the pattern and create a new behavioural response. Imagine if your team started using this language, if they were able to identify when they were overthinking things, putting too much meaning on to what stakeholders on their projects might be thinking. Imagine what resource would be freed up if we were better able to manage the collective worries of our teams – how valuable would that be?

To summarise this chapter, we have specific areas in the brain dedicated to seeing. We see our world every minute of every day that we are awake. We can interpret billions of bits of data. Yet even though we have specific parts of the brain dedicated to this task – *we still get it wrong*.

What else are we getting wrong?

If we consider the perceptual illusions as a metaphor for generally how we are interpreting our world, surely other illusions must exist: cognitive illusions, decision-making illusions, and so on. We aren't as good at things as we think we are. We aren't as objective as we judge ourselves to be. Therefore, we need to be open to the fact that sometimes how we are seeing and interpreting our world, events, and situations around us might be wrong.

To do this, we need to raise our self-awareness. Given that our experiences and our perceptions ultimately shape how we interpret the world and the meaning we give to it, it makes sense to know as much about ourselves as possible. It's important to know who we are, what we believe, and how we respond to things.

Why? Because all these elements affect our perception of the world and ultimately the decisions we make. It's the culmination of all our decisions that determines our results in life.

If you consider that our perception is a lens through which we view the world, then it is true that if you change your perception you can change how you see and interpret your world. In other words, if you change your perception, you can change your world.

Understanding our emotions, our values and our beliefs is critical. Being able to view them and understand the impact of each of those, how they play on each other and how they produce very many different outcomes. These things aren't separate, they are all interlinked and connected, but it's helpful for us to think of them separately as then they are easier concepts to comprehend.

– *Dr David Wilkinson, Editor-in-Chief of the* Oxford Review

All actions are preceded by thoughts and feelings. Therefore my thoughts and feelings are as real, and in some ways more important, than the actions that will flow from them. So in my business, every action I will take during the day is preceded by thoughts and feelings. It's illogical, if not dangerous, for me to not be mindful and aware of those thoughts and feelings that are compelling my actions every day.

– *Matthew McCarthy, CEO, Ben & Jerry's*

5 The Stories We Tell Ourselves

We all tell ourselves stories about the events we experience in everyday life. The meaning that we give to a situation, an object, or event is influenced by three elements:

1. Content: What information is held within the situation, object, or event?

2. Context: What other information is surrounding this scene?

3. Experience: When have I seen this before? When might I have experienced this before? What can I learn from my memories? What can I learn from the past?

Reminding ourselves of what we've learned from the visual illusions in the previous chapter and applying it to the cognitive illusions that might be showing up in our lives, we now know that how we are perceiving the world, and our lack of awareness of our cognitive illusions, can often lead to self-imposed restrictions.

Whether we're aware of it or not, all of us keep a running account of what's happening to us, what it means, and what we think we should do as a result. We practise scenarios in our heads. We future-pace ourselves. In other words, our minds are constantly monitoring, interpreting, and deciding what anything means at any given moment. It's how we stay on track and how we make sense of the world around us.

The challenge is that, depending on where our heads are in the moment, we can get things wrong – and we don't recognise that we are getting it wrong.

Some people can put extreme interpretations on the things that happen and then react in an exaggerated way. They may have exaggerated feelings of anxiety, happiness, or anger.

We've all been there, and we know people who are like that – a little melodramatic, for good or for bad. The fact is that absolutely nothing has inherent meaning. As Shakespeare said in *Hamlet*, 'There is nothing either good or bad, but thinking makes it so.' How many narratives are shared but unspoken within your teams? What resistance might it be creating? What would be possible if those narratives became visible and you could actually work towards overcoming them? In the chapter on beliefs, we will show you exactly how you can do this to unlock the performance of the teams you work within.

> You come into the world with all kinds of assumptions and biases, they're ingrained in the functional architecture of your brain .... We are given information, it is without meaning, it's what we do with that information that matters.
>
> – *Beau Lotto, a leading neuroscientist and expert in perception*

What happens to us and what we think that means are two different things. It's the story we tell ourselves that creates the end result. Here are some examples of this that could play out in the workplace:

- My boss looked angry when I asked for a day's holiday; it's because he doesn't want me to go.
- My friend didn't call back; it's because they're mad at me.
- Someone yawned during my talk; it's because I'm bad at speaking.

- My dad asked about my weekend – it's because he thinks I'm always partying and not working hard enough.

How about …

You call a colleague about an issue with an important project that will affect the deadline; no answer.

You leave a message.

Some time passes with no reply. You think about it, maybe you worry a little, maybe you start to overthink.

You start thinking that they're upset with you.

Then you start generating possible things they're annoyed about; you mention it to other colleagues.

They're more senior than you, so you start to worry what they think about you.

Have you offended them in some way? Should you have talked to them in person instead of calling? You re-read the email exchanges from the past week to check if there was something that might have been misconstrued.

Then you start to get annoyed with *them* for not following up. You build up evidence in your head for how they're being 'rude' – you turn the tables from being insecure to being angry!

We've all been there.

But nothing happened. Literally nothing happened!

You made a call, and nothing happened. Everything else has been created in your mind. Someone not returning your call could mean something. Or it could mean NOTHING. Perhaps they never got the message, or they intended to call back and had been very busy, or they prefer to arrange a meeting to discuss it in detail with the whole team.

Pay attention to the 'story' we tell ourselves, because it's this story that affects how we feel and influences our decisions – for good and bad.

Figure 5.1   Fact to fantasy.

These 'stories' we tell ourselves tend to progress from facts to 'faction' (a bit of fact and a bit of fiction). The more we elaborate and the further from the event we move, the more fiction comes into play. We build things up and up and with the help of other people's stories, we soon move to fantasy (Figure 5.1), but all the while we think we are still in the realm of 'fact'.

Event + Response = Outcome

Let me share with you a simple equation to help you remember everything we've covered. I learned this from Jack Canfield, who has written *The Success Principles*, *Chicken Soup for the Soul* and many other books on personal development. If you haven't read those, I highly recommend them.

The equation is $E + R = O$ (see Figure 5.2). We have an ***event*** and then our ***response*** and finally the ***outcome***. Many things happen in our lives and I am sure you've heard yourself and other people say things like, 'My boss really frustrates me', or, 'That waitress got our order wrong and it just ruined the night', or, 'That person really, really annoys me.'

Your ability to respond
is based on the meaning we give to things.

You have a CHOICE.

Event   **Response**   Outcome

"If you always do what you've always done,
you'll always get what you've always got."

Jack Canfield, The Success Principles

Figure 5.2   E + R = O.

You're deceiving yourself, because it's not actually what's happening. Something happens: you go for a business dinner, and the waitress gets your order wrong. You have decided that your response is anger and that she has ruined the night. But you have a choice. You have a choice of story you decide to tell yourself. She didn't make you angry. You've decided to be angry; that is the emotion that you've chosen as your response. It all gets exaggerated, and suddenly she's ruined the night. You cannot control the event, but you *can* control your response to it, which subsequently will influence the outcome. The R is for RESPONSE, because if you think of the word 'responsibility', it means your *ability* to *respond*.

You have a choice.

Let me tell you briefly about the story of Viktor Frankl to bring this to life. Some of you may know of him; some of you may not. He was a concentration camp survivor, and when he was interned, he was surrounded by people suffering, people losing hope, people losing the will to live. Even after years, he continued to always have strength. His job while he was in the camp was a shocking one: to remove the bodies from the gas chambers. We can't imagine the things that he witnessed and experienced.

He went into the concentration camps with his family, and he removed them from the gas chambers. If anyone had an excuse to be angry, disappointed, and enraged with the world, to have no hope to go on, it was he.

But he didn't give up; he stayed strong. He actually became an inspiration not only to the other prisoners, but to the prison guards. He was lucky enough to still be alive when the war came to an end, and he was released. After learning about Viktor Frankl, I watched an interview with him on YouTube,[1] and you can check it out yourself. He has been asked by many people how on earth was he able to respond the way he did? How did he keep his power and strength and act with his humility intact?

His answer: 'Simple, but it wasn't easy.' Everything had been taken from him … his identity, his family, all the people that he had ever loved, and he had nothing. The only thing he realised he had was a choice over how he was going to let these events affect him and his life. He decided that he was going to find the lesson in everything that happened to him. When he was being tortured, he cast himself in his mind's eye to a lecture hall in the United States because he imagined that if he got out of there alive, he was going to tell the world what mankind could learn from such atrocities.

He would project himself in his mind's eye, and take the learning in every situation to share later, and that's what kept him alive.

---

[1] https://www.youtube.com/watch?v=UgVA6nXCj1U

He chose a different response. He chose to learn from the events in his life.

If he can do that with that sort of trauma, we can do that when our boss annoys us, when our partner irritates us, when a waitress gets our order wrong … whatever it might be. All it takes is the time to step back and recognise that we have a choice and a response. Then we can truly take control of our lives. We can influence the outcome.

You can't change the event, but you can change your response, and instead of spiralling out of control, you can choose a better, more positive story. You can choose to give people the benefit of the doubt and, as a result, the experience of your life will be different and more positive as well. So, remember, you can't choose the event, but you can choose the response. By changing the response, you can change the outcomes in life.

This is helpful for small patterns that appear in your life too. What stories might you have going on right now in your life? Maybe about your capability? About what your team thinks of you as a leader? Perhaps about your chances of promotion? How much worth and value do you contribute to the team or the company?

We all have these types of thoughts lurking in the backs of our minds. Everyone you work with does. It's when they aren't helpful yet remain unchallenged that they become a problem. When I work with teams that have unhealthy dynamics, there are usually 'stories' perpetuating in the team that aren't necessarily true. If they linger, they can cause ongoing problems.

A couple of years ago I was working with a senior leadership team in a law firm. I had come in to work with the team about eight weeks after the previous leader of the team had been 'removed'. Unfortunately, there had been what can only be described as psychological and emotional bullying occurring. The company had assumed that when the aggressor was removed, the team would be relieved and return to health as long as a good leader was put in the post. An extremely good leader had been put into the position, but the team was damaged.

I ran one-to-one confidential interviews with each team member to understand what more was going on. What transpired was that there were two camps within the team: the old camp, which had been poorly treated for a long period of time, and the new camp, which were seen as the favourites of the outgoing leader.

There was a lot of mistrust between the two camps; they had created stories about each other, resulting in greater distance and divides within the team. I brought them together for a three-day team workshop, with the objective of getting this team back to a place of health. Our first day was focused on putting them all on the same page. I had everyone sit in a circle and I debriefed the research, which allowed me to point at the elephant in the room. I shared the fact that both parties were in pain and that both were suffering under the weight of the 'stories' that each camp had created about the other. I then shared both sides of the narrative that each camp had developed. I also explained why people create such stories (safety, making sense of what's happening, creating shared viewpoints, common enemy, etc.).

After sharing both sides of the narrative (which I did completely anonymously, meaning I could keep a sense of psychological safety in the room), I then invited anyone who wanted to respond to speak. There was silence for the first few moments, but then the first person spoke, a long-standing member of the team, and she said it was the first time she had considered that the other camp was hurting, too.

Someone from the other side spoke and said they genuinely had no idea of how much the older team members had suffered. There was a collective sigh of relief in the room as both camps realised they were just a group of hurt people trying to navigate a toxic and difficult situation.

It was this realisation that opened up everyone's 'perception' of what was happening and allowed them to step aside from the narrative they had created to seek the truth. This was the beginning of what was set to be probably one of the more emotional (and delicate!) but rewarding sessions I have run with a team. The impact was profound.

This is the power of recognising that our perception is biased and that we add meaning (sometimes helpful, sometimes not) that isn't always there. Often, just helping teams realise that we have this added layer between us can be enough to remove its power.

This story illustrates the power of a shared narrative, which if left unquestioned, can create greater divides among people than is necessary.

There are a set of emotions that you're allowed at work, and a set that you're not allowed. There's a way of being; people would not feel comfortable, for example, crying in the boardroom. So they disappear and remove themselves from whatever it happens to be. We know from a personal point of view the result of suppression and its negativity on our health. Through research, we're starting to see what institutional suppression of emotions is and the effect that it's having on effective decision making in companies. We need to address this and we can do so through education on emotional and social intelligence.

– Dr David Wilkinson, Editor-in-Chief of the Oxford Review

6 Everything Is Connected

N ow let's discover the impact of such narratives on us internally –
how our thinking affects our emotions and subsequently our
actions. This is often referred to as the mind-body connection, and
when we understand it, we can 'hack' it to our advantage.

What's fascinating is that until the 1800s, most doctors believed
that emotions were linked to disease and advised patients to visit spas
or seaside resorts when they were ill. But with the advancement of
medical science, the focus soon shifted to antibiotics and surgery. We
abandoned the notion of how our feelings can have an overall effect
on our sense of well-being.

Interestingly, society has recently started to investigate the connection once more. I have a number of friends who are nurses and
doctors, and they have shared with me that in the UK, in around
2013, they introduced new modules in the standard nursing bache-
lor's degree called 'The Psychology of Illness', where they studied how
our feelings (specifically negative ones) could contribute to ill health
in the body.

I'm not suggesting we enter the debate on illness. Instead I'm interested in sharing how our internal influences affect us personally (in a
less detrimental way, but also in an important way that we need to
acknowledge). I want to illustrate this for you through a simple dia-
gram (Figure 6.1).

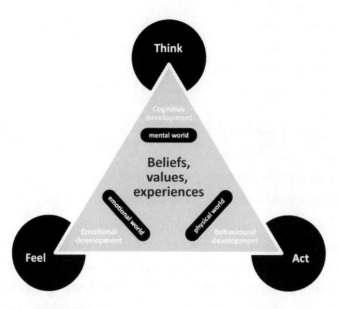

Figure 6.1 Internal impacts.

If you look at the three corners, you'll see that our emotional development is in one corner, behavioural development in another, and our cognitive development is in the final corner. Of course, this separation is for illustrative purposes only. We are complex and layered in real life; the model is just that, a 'model', designed to help us talk about these different aspects of the self. The model is drawing attention to our emotional world, our physical world, and our mental world, and is found in the foundations of cognitive behavioural therapy.

Our emotional world is, as you'd expect, about how we feel. Our cognitive world is about what we think, and our behavioural world is about how we act. These are all interconnected and entwined, but many of us act as if they are separate and autonomous.

So, how are they connected? Well, when we think a thought, it makes us feel a certain way, and that can impact how we act. Let's use my earlier example of asking your boss for a vacation and receiving a strange look in response. You think to yourself, *'My boss is maybe annoyed with me about something or maybe they are in a bad mood'*.

You might then experience a mixture of feelings. You could feel frustrated or annoyed with your boss, or you could feel hurt or upset. You could feel disappointed, and depending on how you feel, you're going to act a certain way. Maybe you'll avoid them, maybe you won't answer the next time they call, maybe you'll go back to your desk and complain to your friends; whatever you do, it all has an effect. Again, this is because of the meaning that you have overlaid onto that 'look', which made you feel something, which in turn made you think something, and as a result you acted and behaved in a certain way.

I've deliberately used a personal example to help you connect to the point. But now let's apply it to the business. Imagine you're working on a disruptive innovation project for your brand, but deep down, you think that you're never going to come up with anything unique or different. What does that do to how you feel? Most likely you'll feel demotivated, that the project is futile, or you'll just have a low-level scepticism playing in the background of your mind. How will that impact your behaviours? Well, you might not be willing to push your creative boundaries because you don't quite buy into what's possible. When you brief agencies to support on the challenge, you may not be convincing, inspiring, or motivating. You'll say all the right things, but there's a difference when someone *believes* in what they're saying. Moving forward, you might be more risk averse (because what's the point, if you don't fully buy into the possibility?); you might not invest in the innovation workshop to the degree you should, and instead do something half-hearted. In the end it will be self-fulfilling, because that thought impacted your feelings and subsequently your behaviours.

This is why it's so important to tune into your thinking and also share it upfront (before it becomes too much of a mental obstacle). Anytime we work with teams on their big vision or purpose, we always have a session where we tear it apart. Because we want to get everybody's innermost fears, worries, and doubts out on the table – so we can all see them. Because when you see the hidden obstacles lurking in people's minds, you can work with them. When you can't see them, that's when they cause the most damage to the goals we're trying to achieve. This is what I mean when I talk about the Hidden Edge – if we're not paying attention to our mental game (and that of our team's), there can be hidden resistance working against us that no one is aware of. Equally, when we tap into our mental game and seek to enhance our mental fitness, that's when we see performance peak. More on that later.

Now, back to the model. There isn't a one-way system around the triangle. It works in lots of different ways.

If you're feeling tired, it's going to have an impact on how you think. We know this, but we usually ignore it. Let's take, for example, a Sunday morning. You've worked a chunk of the weekend, then maybe had a couple of glasses of wine to 'switch off', maybe you are a bit tired and your energy is depleted. What usually happens on Sundays?

Well, we tend to be a little more fragile as often we've not rested enough, and Monday is already looming. Because of these factors, the quality of our thinking also isn't that good. It has been compromised. Often, we have a tendency to feel worse about things that we wouldn't normally feel that bad about. In this scenario, you'll worry about work the next day and will be a little bit more anxious than usual.

Things will feel bigger than they normally do, and you're going to act a little bit differently as a result. That might mean you lie on the sofa, energy depleted, or you look at your agenda for the week and feel a bit stressed by it. All of these aspects are influencing each other. You feel a certain way (tired/fragile), which has led to a more negative/anxious quality to your thinking, which is making you behave a certain way (worrying about work/not sleeping well).

If you're in a bad mood, frustrated by something that happened at work or at home, more than likely you will have higher doses of cortisol flowing through your body. This is the 'stress hormone' secreted by your adrenal glands. We can try and 'think' our way out of that mood, but it's much quicker to *feel* our way out. How?

Often by simply listening to your favourite band/singer, talking about an amazing holiday you had with a friend, putting on a comedy or your favourite movie, doing some yoga, meditating. In short, laughing, exercising, and breathing slowly will all help release oxytocin into your bloodstream.

Oxytocin is a neurohypophyseal hormone produced by the hypothalamus and secreted by the posterior pituitary gland. It increases the feeling of trust and produces an overall positive sense of well-being. The good news is you can hack the mind-body connection to get you feeling, thinking, and acting in a more beneficial way.

You can 'hack' anywhere on the triangle. Starting with behaviour, if you change what you are *doing*, this will have an impact on what you are *thinking* and how you are *feeling*. For example, if you're frustrated in the office, *get out*; go for a walk outside in the sunlight. Change your overall environment: stand instead of sitting, run around the block, etc. These small actions can boost the *serotonin* in your body. This chemical is a neurotransmitter that has many functions within the human body. Some researchers believe it is responsible for maintaining mood balance and that a deficit of serotonin can lead to depression.

Four ways to boost serotonin activity are:

• Sunlight
• Massage
• Exercise
• Remembering happy events

Consider if you're about to present your project to investors, or you are trying to get through an important 'gate' (perhaps to get the next stage of investment). Consider you're about to present your project to investors, or you are trying to get through an important 'gate' (perhaps to get the next stage of investment). If you're walking into that room nervous, having not slept well, on your third espresso, how do you think it's going to go? I always encourage people to unlock their internal pharmacy before 'performing', whether it's doing jumping jacks, listening to some pumped-up music, or fuelling your body properly (ideally all three) – you are accessing your inner resources to enhance your outer performance. You need to always make sure you are playing for yourself, not *against* yourself.

With the mind-body connection, I've given you an example of how your thinking can affect your feelings, which then affect your actions. I've also given you an example of how your feelings can affect your thinking and subsequently your actions.

Let me now share how your behaviour can influence how you feel and what you think. In the West, we have a tendency to try and think ourselves in and out of situations. We're very thinky-thinky. And if you're in a bad mood, what can you do to make yourself feel better? You can try and 'think' your way out of it, but it's not easy. You could instead decide to call a friend and have a good conversation. But there's a trick we can use to short-circuit all of that: we can use our body to actually make us feel better and think better.

For instance, when you do exercise, how do you feel afterwards? You feel great, because endorphins are going through your body. Dopamine kicks in and floods you with good feelings. You've just accessed your natural, internal pharmacy. It's very difficult to feel bad after a workout. You generally feel good. Another 'hack' you can use is to put your favourite music on, because music is a shortcut to enhancing your feelings. If you put on your favourite song, often you automatically feel a little bit better, and that will influence how you think, which will influence how you act. It's a powerful life hack.

We have a tendency to disconnect our brains from our feelings and our actions, whether we acknowledge it or not. Below is a quick summary of what we've covered so far.

Our Thoughts Affect Our Feelings

If we are in a self-conscious or negative loop, it will influence our emotions similarly.

For example, thinking 'I'm not ready' before a pitch presentation can make us feel anxious, nervous, and insecure. This in turn affects how we then perform: we might stumble over our words, have a shaky voice, etc.

Our Feelings Affect Our Thoughts

If we feel energised and happy, it skews the quality of our thinking also to the positive.

For example, we tend to display more gratitude and are more likely to interpret ambiguous scenarios by 'giving people the benefit of the doubt' versus thinking the worst of them.

Both Our Feelings and Our Emotions Affect Our Behavior, and Vice Versa

We make different decisions based on what we think and feel (whether we are conscious of it or not) which leads to different actions. The opposite is also true, if we've just exercised, or watched something funny and someone asks us to do something that might have an element of risk. We are much more likely to diminish the risk in our minds because we are in a good mood (the movement will have released some endorphins, and the laughter will have enhanced your social bonding) and say yes.

We've explored the corners of the triangle, but what's in the middle? It's our past experiences, our beliefs, and our values. All of these are influences that you may or may not be aware of, and we will cover those in the following chapters. Our personal experiences can also influence everything, from our careers and our approach to business to our relationships and opinions about our capabilities.

These influences can be grouped into present and past.

The Present

- Internal factors: Physiology – what is happening in our body (relaxed, centred, tired, hungry, all underpinned by hormones such as adrenaline, DHEA)
- External factors: Society, economy, weather, politics

The Past

- Our experiences
- Our beliefs (shaped by our past experiences)

When we think about the **future**, it's fair to say that it should be a blank canvas, that anything is possible. The problem for many of us is that our past is already in our future. By that I mean the experiences that we've had in the past can affect our choices in the future. The experiences that we had when we were at the beginning of our career can affect the decisions that we make today about our future career.

This is why it's so important to unpack the experiences that we bring to the table. They don't have to be big, challenging things. They can be small events that have shaped our view and expectations of the world, ultimately affecting what we believe and where we spend our thinking time.

That's really what mental fitness is all about. It's about helping us tune in to who we really are, our typical thinking patterns, our usual emotional responses, and our behaviours. This is not just about who we are, but who we want to become. Some of the beliefs we have picked up along the way are not true; they also aren't helpful and may be holding us back in life and in business.

Through this book, I want to help you get to know who you are and which beliefs you want to keep, as well as which beliefs to challenge and shed. This works for individuals and for teams. It's this clarity, this self-awareness, that can awaken us to the endless possibilities within our future (and the mental obstacles in our way). We have much more power over who we are and how we react to the world than we give ourselves credit for.

Why am I telling you all of this? I'm telling you because truly acknowledging that our thoughts, emotions and behaviours are all connected can be enough to raise your awareness and get you to begin to question the daily influences affecting your performance in life and in business.

My request to you is to pay attention to how your thinking (and your team's thinking) affects emotions and behaviours (and vice versa). With this awareness, you can begin to uncover the hidden obstacles holding you and your team back. Not only that, but you can replace some of those thoughts and feelings for ones which will motivate and inspire you forward, helping you overcome unexpected challenges, be creative in the face of setbacks, and agile when dealing with change.

One way of looking at what we're doing is about accessing the inner resources of a human being as a source of competitive advantage and a source of fulfilment. The aspects of personal mastery are being present, creating space, showing yourself, vulnerability, and being compassionate and direct. It's about creating inner space, knowing your emotions and even being able to notice that you have contradictory emotions is totally fine; it's very healthy in fact. It's about raising your awareness of those things.

The key is to manage the integration of the tensions that we might be facing. As a company, Unilever has integrated our model of leadership, what we call the 'Standards of Leadership'. It's knowledge that we've always had, that there's something about some people that just helps them lead. We've integrated that into a model which has really helped us. Knowing that it is the work that we do on our inner game that can fuel our outer game is key.

— Tim Munden, Chief Learning Officer, Unilever

Talking about and encouraging mental fitness (not just mental wellness or health) is a new paradigm. We now know that it's the mental game that gives us an edge in life and in business. I was trained as one of the best snipers in the world, coming from being a very alpha male Royal Marine Commando. I breathe, I control my thoughts, I control the controllables, I try not to lose my temper. The Commando spirit is about courage, determination, unselfishness and cheerfulness in the face of adversity — this is actually all about our mental game; it's mental fitness.

— Aldo Kane, Adventurer, Record Setter
and former Royal Marines Commando

7 Emotion and Decision Making

All of the elements we've been discussing – our emotional world, our physical world, and our mental world – act as filters on perception. I've begun drawing your attention to your thinking, but there is much more work to be done. Another area where we are starved of knowledge and understanding is the topic of emotions.

What has become clear – both in my own work and acknowledged by others in the field – is that many adults (and children) do not have emotional literacy. This means the ability to accurately acknowledge and label your emotions. Brené Brown, a shame and vulnerability researcher who works with leaders in major companies across the world, has been capturing data on this topic for many years. She has asked 15 000 adults over the last seven years who go through her curriculum to name as many emotions as possible, ones that they can recognise in themselves and name and/or recognise in others. The mean number of emotions that people can identify and name is three. People have little training in emotions.

On the next page are some examples of emotions explained by Dr Marc Brackett (Director, Yale Center for Emotional Intelligence, and author of *Permission to Feel*) to help you enhance your own literacy. The challenge is the shared assumption that we know what emotions mean and we know how to describe them, but it's really important to accurately define them, which many of us are missing.

Anger	Perceived injustice
Envy	Wanting what someone else wants/has
Disappointment	Unmet expectations
Jealousy	Feeling threatened
Joy	Achieving a goal

Understanding That Our Emotions Matter

Emotions matter much more than most of us realise. They influence our ability to focus. If we are feeling bullied, insecure, or fearful, often we cannot focus or concentrate and are distracted. Our emotional systems are inextricably linked to our cognitive processes.

Dr Marc Brackett ran an experiment with teachers. He randomly assigned them to be in a good mood or a bad mood, which only required them to take five minutes and think about a good day or a bad day. Then he got each teacher to grade *exactly* the same paper. There was one to two full grades' difference between the teachers in a good mood and those in a bad mood. When he asked the teachers, 'Do you believe that the way you felt had any influence over the way you graded the paper?' 90% of them said, 'No'.

Their emotions clearly shifted the way they viewed the same content, but they didn't want to believe it. Why? Because it makes us feel as though we don't have any control.

Emotions affect our physical and mental health. In further research conducted by Dr Brackett with educators, he found that the culture and climate of a school was highly correlated with the anxiety and stress of its teachers, which was also correlated with the teachers' mental health problems, sleep problems, and their body mass index. Our emotional system and our environment are closely linked, and these, in turn, are connected to our mental health. This is also true of our businesses and the teams running our brands.

There's another way in which our emotions affect our lives. In his paper 'Psychology of Aesthetics Creativity and the Arts', Dr Brackett says

> So many people (and our children) do not reach their full potential because they can't deal with the feedback they get, they can't deal with the disappointment, the anxiety, and the frustration "around" the content. It's not their ability to be creative that's an issue, it's when they fail at it or they get harsh feedback they can't deal with the feelings around it. They give up, not because of their ability, but because of their inability to deal with their feelings.[1]

I think this quote is fascinating. How many projects in our businesses don't see the light of day because our teams can't handle failure and so give up? I regularly hear leaders saying 'fail fast', 'experiment', and 'progress over perfection', but the truth is, if the system doesn't support this ethos (e.g. if you won't get your bonus because your product launch was not as successful as forecasted), then you will never encourage the behaviour you want to see. If we want innovation, to disrupt the marketplace, to 'fail fast', we need to do three fundamental things:

1. We need to nurture and encourage risk taking and help people manage the natural anxiety and worry surrounding that.

2. We need to teach people (and have them practice) how to be OK with failure. Not only that, but how to live with the emotions surrounding failure and how to not absorb it as part of their identity.

3. The system needs to encourage points 1) and 2); in other words, the ecosystem they are working within should be strong in feelings of psychological safety. The metrics by which people are measured should positively reward risk takers, experimenters, and those truly learning from doing (which means those who are failing).

---

[1] Ivcevic Pringle, Z. and Brackett, M. A. (2015, November) 'Psychology of Aesthetic Creativity and the Arts', *American Psychological Association*, 9 (4): 480–487.

The focus must be as much on 'how' people are working as on the final outcome (market share/margin, etc.).

George Loewenstein, who wrote a paper titled 'Emotions of Economic Theory and Economic Behavior', has been quoted as saying:

Our many emotions, anger, fear, etc., impact our behaviour just like our drive states: hunger, thirst, sexual desire.[2]

If we are emotionally charged – often described as a 'hot state' – it's going to affect our decision-making process. That's a very powerful statement. 'Hot states' refer to times when you're anxious, angry, very excited, etc. We have empirical evidence that they affect our decisions, but we rarely adjust for the fact that we are in a 'hot state'. To give you an example, I remember a few years ago working on-site at the head office of one our biggest clients. I was at the coffee machine, and there was a real buzz of hushed whispers and nervousness. As I knew the people, I asked them what was going on. That day was the monthly gate-keeping meeting where the senior leadership team would meet project teams. Each team would present updates on their projects, latest consumer research results etc. If the project was at a key milestone they would be asking for sign off from the leaders to move forward. The head of the leadership team was clearly having a bad day, and at one point went on a rant and threw a book across the room. Nobody knew what to do. The project team took the verbal slamming they got and left the room. That's when I met them at the coffee machine, when they were buzzing on adrenaline and licking their wounds. Now, we could go into a discussion about emotions in the boardroom and so on, but I don't want to go down that rabbit hole. What I think is more important is what happened next. Every single project team that went into that decision-making forum, for the rest of the day, got challenged, interrogated, and criticised. Regardless of why the senior leader

---

[2]Loewenstein, G. (2000) 'Emotions in Economic Theory and Economic Behavior', *American Economic Review*, 90 (2): 426–432.

was in a bad mood and whether it was justified, it cast a shadow over the rest of the day. But more importantly, it will have cost the business an incalculable amount of money, because projects didn't meet key milestones, they didn't get CapEx signed off; they got sent back to the drawing board on pack designs, advertising campaigns, and supply chain challenges. This was all because the senior leader was unable (or unwilling) to manage their emotions and acknowledge his hot state was going to negatively influence every decision made that day.

The leadership team should have called a break. The senior leader should have taken himself out of the scenario, walked around the block, got some fresh air, had a conversation to help reframe his thinking and emotions, etc. If he had rebalanced, the meeting could have resumed; if not, it should have been postponed. But instead, everyone ignored what was happening and continued as usual. When you are mentally and emotionally fit, you have the self-awareness to know when you need to take yourself out of a situation and 'reset'.

When these situations happen with ourselves and our teams, we need to practise and role-model stepping back from the situation and considering what else is going on. If you are the one in the hot state, it's good to ask yourself the question: What's going on with me and how is that affecting my thinking, my feeling, and my decisions? If you think it's having an influence, then this tells you that you need to avoid making further key decisions at that moment until you can reset yourself.

Based on his research, Dr Marc Brackett has introduced a simple yet powerful tool into school systems in the United States. It's so effective that I think everyone should be using it, not just children. It's called RULER, which is an acronym. When you pause to reflect, the RULER technique will help you check in with yourself:

- R – Recognise emotions in oneself and others (pay attention to cues in your body and mind, observing behaviour and body language in others).

- U – Understand emotion: know the causes and consequences of feelings.

- L – Label emotion (correctly).

- E – Express (communicate how you feel in a healthy way).

- R – Regulate – enhance, reduce, prevent, create, maintain, etc. (utilising strategies to regulate feelings).

Our moods are an obvious influence because we have all been in a situation where we are in a good mood and it makes us more inclined to agree with someone, to brainstorm, to do something that maybe we wouldn't normally do.

Mood completely influences our decisions. When we are in a good mood, we rely much more on intuition.[3] We don't need all of the facts, nor do we need all of the information. What's actually happening is a reduction in critical thought and a reduction in focus on detail. We are much more likely to be spontaneous in making decisions. When we are in a good mood, it makes us much more receptive to new information.

We can apply this to our jobs: if we are about to go into a creative ideation session or a high-stakes, very senior pitch, ideally put on your favourite music, go for a run or a walk around the building before you start because it will open up your mind and help with agile thinking and learning. These are fast and effective ways of hacking our performance. We know emotions affect our performance but most of us aren't leveraging it.

Getting ourselves into a positive mood is optimal for performance because when we are in a bad mood or in not such a good place, the mind shuts down, and our creative abilities are limited. We are less likely to take risks. We're also much less likely to absorb new information.[4]

---

[3] Isen, A. M. and Means, B. (1983) 'The Influence of Positive Affect on Decision-Making Strategy', *Social Cognition*, 2 (1).
[4] Schwarz, N. (2000) 'Emotion, Cognition, and Decision Making', *Cognition and Emotion*, 14 (4): 433–440.

Have You Ever Been 'Hangry'?

Let's talk about how physiological states can affect how we view the world and the meaning that we give to it. I'm sure that you have experienced being 'hangry'. In case you haven't heard the term before, it's where hunger meets anger. We've all been in a situation where someone might be irritating us or frustrating us a little bit; it often happens in long meetings or workshops, and we see ourselves getting more annoyed than usual.

What we haven't noticed is that we skipped lunch, and our hunger is actually amplifying our feelings. It's the hunger that's making us irritable, not necessarily the person talking, but we have misattributed it to them. It's so common that it's been given the name 'hangry' in popular culture. I'm sure you've experienced it. I've gotten myself into arguments before from being hungry! Then, when I eat, my nervous system calms down, and I realise I'm not as worked up as I was before. This is why we should pay attention not only to the things that are happening around us, but also to what is happening within us.

We need to be aware of our physiological state as much as our emotions. Are we tired? Are we sick? Are we hungry? Are we anxious? This is affecting how we see the world, and it will be affecting the quality of our thinking and subsequently affecting our behaviour and the decisions that we make. This becomes even more crucial in a business environment where we might be making major decisions that could cost us money if emotions are getting in the way, going unpoliced and even unnoticed.

The simple truth is that we should avoid making decisions when our physiological state is compromised (unless we really have to). What we need to do first is sort out the physiological state. Always step out of the situation and ask yourself, 'What else is happening? What else is going on around here that I might not be picking up on? Have I been in this situation before? Really, and ideally, you want to be in a neutral place or in a positive place. If things are not quite right with you, don't commit to anything, don't make major decisions, and don't have big important conversations until you're in a more neutral state of emotion and physiology.

This is also true when you need decisions to be made by your team or by senior stakeholders. Is it a good moment to ask them to make a decision? I can guarantee you if it's the end of a long working day where they have been in intense meetings for the last three days, it's probably *not* a good time. Be smart about how and when you seek critical thinking from people, especially in business. The great news about the extraneous variables that might be impacting upon us is that once we are aware of their effects, they can be nullified.

Research conducted by Schwarz and Clore[5] perfectly demonstrates this. They asked a group of participants to rate their overall satisfaction with their lives.

They looked at how their answers correlated with the weather. If it was raining on the day that they asked the question, people were significantly more likely to say that they were not happy with where they were in their lives. By contrast, if it was sunny, they were significantly more likely to say that life was great. When the researchers pointed out the weather to the participants by saying, 'Have you noticed that it's raining today?' or, 'Have you noticed that it's a very lovely day today?', the participants were able to take that into account and say, 'Yeah, actually, maybe that's affecting my answer'. As a result, they were able to adjust for it and recognise that life wasn't as bad as they thought, but instead that they were being unknowingly influenced.

---

[5] Schwarz, N. and Clore, G. L. (1983) 'Mood, Misattribution, and Judgments of Well-Being: Informative and Directive Functions of Affective States', *Journal of Personality and Social Psychology*, 45: 513–523.

Having that awareness alone can liberate us from its influence, which is why, within business, we always need to be paying attention not just to what is happening in front of us, but also to what's happening within and around us.

Applying Learnings to Your Life

If you think about the most inspiring leaders you've come across in your career, or the wise people within your life, you'll notice they all have something in common. When people can't think of anyone immediately, I get them to conjure up characters like Gandalf (*The Lord of the Rings*), Yoda (*Star Wars*), and Dumbledore (*Harry Potter*). What do they have in common? They are centred. They don't fly off the handle or act on emotion. They always look for the bigger picture, they search for the unseen – before reacting. If you can channel a bit of their energy and composure into yourself before reacting, you will most certainly get different results from yourself and from the people you work with. This is ultimately emotional and social intelligence, which is the cornerstone of mental fitness.

Learning to see things differently and thinking differently all begin with awareness and questioning. The problem with questions is that they raise uncertainty in your mind, and evolutionarily speaking, we don't like uncertainty. As I said earlier, we as humans are wired to avoid it because uncertainty brings hesitation, which risks death.

Of course, the threats and predators that we had before are gone. We live in a modern world where it's a lot safer, and we're unlikely to be eaten by a sabre-toothed tiger. Despite this, our survival mechanisms still take control, and our brain and our emotions still react in the same way. This means we need to learn how to retrain our brain for the modern world.

We all need help to challenge our perceptions and the meaning that we give to things. When you begin to question your typical responses, tuning into them and attempting to reprogram them, this is when you will truly grow. I have a simple yet powerful technique to wake you up to the influences that may be affecting you and your team.

It's based on some straightforward questions that you can apply every day in your life to help you to change your perception and see things differently. When you get into the routine, this will become habitual, and you will be able to do it instantly.

You may find yourself in a situation where perhaps you can sense that you're not quite right, not quite sure how to make a decision or you feel your emotions starting to bubble up. This could be happening to you, a member of your team, or even the whole group may be having the same experience (e.g. a meeting getting extremely heated). You need to stop, pause, and ask yourself the simple 'reaction control' questions some of which we covered earlier:

- What else is going on here? Is there a bigger picture I'm not seeing?
- Have I experienced a similar situation in the past? Did I have a negative reaction? Is that what's happening now?
- How was I feeling before this event/situation? Angry, happy, average? Could this be affecting my interpretation of the situation now?
- What's my/the team's physiology like? Am I tired, hungry, sick, or stressed? Is this also affecting my perception?
- Do we have the basics covered? Is there fresh air in the room, have we had adequate breaks? Do we need to change the environment?

If you answered yes to any of those questions, then your perception is being influenced, either by external or internal influences. Either way, you (and possibly the team) need to take space and time before reacting, or be prepared to deal with the consequences. To move forward, you have three options:

1. Give the other person/situation the benefit of the doubt. Assume they have come with the best intentions, and react according to these positive intentions (not your negative interpretation).

2. Remove yourself from the situation, and respond when you are able to say no to all of the questions. If the whole team are affected, it might be a case of 'parking' the topic with a plan to revisit it later.

3. Share what happened (in a non-biased way) with a colleague, and ask for their interpretation to help you reframe your thinking.

Why Understanding Emotions Is Especially Important for Leaders

Brené Brown, says during her podcast interview[6] with Dr Marc Brackett:

> *I have never met a truly transformational leader in my career that did NOT have a deep understanding of their own emotional landscape and the emotional landscape of other people.*

Dr Marc Brackett conducted a study of 15 000 people across the US workforce, asking them about their feelings. He found that 50–60% of the feelings people experienced on a daily basis were negative. However, he also discovered a magic ingredient: the emotional intelligence of leaders. There was a 50% positive difference in inspiration when people worked with emotionally intelligent leaders. Their frustration levels were 30–40% lower, and their intentions to leave their professions were significantly lower.

Most leaders, and employees in general, have the practical skills to make it in their roles. But the truth is, many companies seek graduates

---

[6]Brackett, M. and Brown, B. (2020) 'Permission to feel', Brené Brown <https://brenebrown.com/podcast/dr-marc-brackett-and-brene-on-permission-to-feel/>

who are proactive problem solvers, creative thinkers, and able to manage conflict with ease. They're looking for people who can inspire and influence others, as well as understand the politics of a company and how to navigate them. These skills simply aren't being taught in most academic systems. Not only that, but they're also often not being taught in companies. Thankfully, I'm lucky enough to work with corporate clients who fully understand that business happens because of the ability of people leveraging these subtleties. As such, we run capabilities training on such topics as navigating conflict, how to manage difficult people, influencing with integrity, and so on. How powerful would it be to bring this training into the education system? I was lucky enough to be trained in my early twenties but only because my degree was in psychology combined with interpersonal communications. Most people don't get the chance to be exposed to such topics, never mind get proficient in them.

More and more, the business world is recognising that the skills we need to cultivate are to do with *how* we show up and *how* we do business, not just *what* we do. But very few people are learning the *how*. When you do the mental fitness work in understanding yourself, the inner workings of your mindset, emotions, thinking, beliefs, values, and so on, you are much better placed to apply that understanding to your relationships with others. This is the essence of emotional and social intelligence – understanding and regulating the self, understanding and managing others. It is this work that helps people manage stressful boardroom situations and allows execs to have hard conversations when they matter most.

In Brené Brown's global work with leaders ('Dare to Lead' programmes), she defines 'courageous leadership' as requiring the ability to attend to fears and feelings. As mentioned during her *Unlocking Us* podcast with Dr Marc Brackett, when she shares this, she says many leaders resist, saying things like, 'I'm not a therapist, I'm a strategist, I don't need to work with fears and feelings'. She then typically asks, 'Tell me your biggest struggle in business, what is your biggest time suck?' They say, 'Dealing with problematic behaviours'. As Brown puts it:

"You can either spend a reasonable time dealing with fears and feelings or an unreasonable time dealing with problematic behaviours."

If leaders can develop their own emotional and social skills to not only understand themselves, but also help them work through some of the hard stuff (fears and feelings) with their teams upfront, it can save a copious amount of hidden 'drag' in the system later on.

As Dr Marc Brackett says: 'As leaders, we need to be preventionists, not interventionists'.

So far, I've explain the neurosceince of vision and demonstrated how our mind can play tricks on us. We used perceptual illusions to bring this to life and to also show you that we have cognitive and emotional illusions happening in our lives too (but we often don't see them). I've shared how we overlay meaning onto things, sometimes helpful meaning, sometimes unhelpful. I've also raised your awareness to the different influences (internal and external) that can impact that meaning. Just now, we've explored emotions and business. In the next chapter, I want to talk to you specifically about how the meaning that we overlay onto events and situations can affect the quality of our thinking.

Authentic leadership is the top trait at the moment that seems in correlation with performance. It's how you get the best results. It's how you breed the most purposeful, supportive, productive team. Being authentic means having high self-awareness and the ability to navigate your thoughts and emotions. We know that the authentic system works. The more authentic an organisation is, the better the wellbeing of its people.

– Marcus Hunt, Head of Global Health Services, EMEA,
Johnson & Johnson

Everything hinges on how my mental state is. If my mental state is clouded, my productivity is impacted, then my mood swings are larger and I'm also blocked off to opportunity. So, simply being in a bit of a rut has an impact on my entire life. It's my mental and emotional fitness that gets me out of that, nothing else.

– Aldo Kane, Adventurer, Record Setter and former Royal
Marines Commando

Part Three
Owning Our Thinking

I n this part, I'm going to get you to think more about your thinking, which is also known as meta-thinking. Through the exercises and information I'll share in the coming chapters, I'll help you tune into your typical thought patterns and enable you to label the thought patterns that might be tripping you up. I refer to these as thinking traps. I'm also going to help you understand what happens neurologically when you fall into a thinking trap and then move into a 'fear response'.

We have a narrative in our minds most of the time, but sometimes the volume of the narrating voice is so low that we aren't conscious it's there, even though it's affecting and influencing us.

This part of the book is designed to turn up the volume on that narrative so that you can understand if it is working for you or against you. The most important point from this section can be encapsulated in just one sentence: *Just because you think a thought, doesn't make it a true.*

However, we often act as if all our thoughts are true. You have to remember that *you* control your thinking; your thinking doesn't control you. This part of the book aims to show you how to take control of your thinking. The first step is to develop awareness and learn how to tune into your thinking. The second step is to be able to label what you notice. This allows you to create distance from your thinking and understand that it is a thought, but it is not *you*, and it's not always representative of truth and fact but more often our insecurities and fears.

When you start to fall into a thinking trap, neurologically and emotionally you activate your fear response, which can affect your behaviour and, of course, your actions and decisions. Every day, you and the people you work with are being influenced by thinking traps. Imagine what is achievable if we all learned how to identify the unhelpful thinking that makes us second-guess ourselves, doubt each other, and not take the steps necessary to execute our plans. A mentally fit team is one that can skilfully navigate the pitfalls of the mind and perform despite them.

8 Navigating Thinking Traps

The monkey trap, traditionally used in some countries, is a glass bowl or coconut husk that has a hole in the middle ... *just* big enough to get a hand in.

Locals put a banana inside and leave it out, near the edge of an overgrowth or jungle, in order to catch a monkey. More often than not, a monkey comes, puts its hand in and grabs the banana. But then when it tries to pull its hand out it can't because the banana stops it.

It seems impossible to get it out.

The monkey will sit there, going backwards and forwards, jumping up and down, making frantic monkey noises all the while holding on to the banana. Then it will see its captors coming and it will start screaming and going crazy. And then a sack goes over its head and it's caught!

All the monkey had to do was let go of the banana to be free ... but it didn't.

Why doesn't the monkey let go of the banana? Because the banana has value, it brings something to the monkey's life.

Just as monkeys are vulnerable to a trap, we too suffer from a 'trap' of our own making!

Our trap is in our minds and stems from our thoughts. Often we don't even realise that we do this to ourselves; we latch onto a thought about something or someone. Usually it is a limiting or a negative thought that can restrict us in our actions or communications. We latch on to that negative thought and instead of us gripping it, it grips us. Just like the monkey, our freedom lies in letting go of that banana, but we can't see it. How would it change your life if you could easily see the cognitive bananas that are trapping you and know to let go? The problem is that, more often than not, we act as though our thoughts are facts. The challenge is to remember that just because we think a thought, that doesn't mean it's true; it doesn't make it a fact.

We control our thoughts; our thoughts do not control us, but too often we act as though it's the other way around. We need to pay more attention to our thinking, sift through our thoughts, and recognise how useful or harmful they can be depending on the circumstances.

Identifying 'Thinking Traps'

It's so important to pay attention to the low-level voice in our heads. This is the voice that tends to narrate what's happening in front of us. When we pay attention, we might hear things like:

'Oh, don't say that thing you're thinking of, it's probably not important and might be wrong, let the others speak instead'.

'If I disagree they might think I'm being rude, better to say nothing'.

'I can't believe I just said that! They're going to think I'm stupid!'

'I can't believe after working all weekend, my boss never replied to my email when I sent the work in' … and so on.

This is often referred to as 'mind chatter'. We all have it going on; for some it's so 'low' they barely notice it. Some of us are more attuned to it than others. Although a few of us have more positive narratives going on, for most of us the voice tends to get louder in our heads when it comes to worry, insecurity, fears, and doubts.

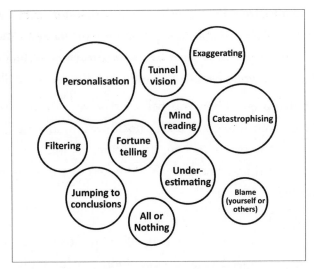

Negative thoughts tend to happen automatically,
half the time you don't even realise they're happening.
The mind has a habit of projecting our fears, many of us
even tend to catastrophise.

Figure 8.1 Common thinking traps.

Have you ever noticed how negative your thoughts can sometimes be; how you often fear the worst, and your thoughts can then easily and quickly spiral out of control? This is why we call them 'thinking traps'. When these negative thoughts go unchecked, unpoliced, and unedited, they can run in the background like a low-playing radio, which can affect your confidence levels and ultimately influence your decisions.

Let me share some common thinking traps (Figure 8.1) that may sound familiar. See if you can find which ones fit you.

How We Create Thinking Traps

Personalisation: Believing that the things others do or say are a direct, personal reaction to you – when it's likely nothing to do with you at all. For example, 'My boss seems irritated and distant today … I must have done something to make them angry with me'. (When in reality they may just be jet-lagged and catching up from that week-long business trip.)

Catastrophising: Exaggerating how badly something will turn out and how you'll be unable to cope with it. For example, 'My doctor asked me to call the office. There must be something wrong with my test results. I just won't be able to handle it if I'm seriously ill'.

Mind Reading: When you believe that you know what others are thinking (even though this isn't possible) and assume the worst. For example, 'She hasn't met me for dinner in weeks even though I've asked three times. She probably thinks I'm annoying now and is avoiding me because of it'.

Filtering: This refers to only paying attention to the negative aspects of a situation while ignoring all the positives. This stops you from drawing a more balanced conclusion. For example, 'My boss looked so bored … My presentation must have been awful!' (Even though other colleagues looked engaged and gave feedback on how useful they found it.)

Tunnel Vision: This is when you just see things one way and you can't see them any other way. Remember the exercise from Chapter 4 with the image that could be an old woman or a young girl? As I explained, often you are only able to see things from one perspective until you are shown another.

Jumping to Conclusions: How many times have you done this? For example, somebody says something, and you decide that it's because they don't like you. You go from one comment straight to a *big* conclusion about that person or often about yourself.

Fortune Telling: 'Well, if I do this then this is going to happen, so therefore, I shouldn't do that … ' In this scenario, it's as if you have a crystal ball and are predicting the future – you can't predict the future.

Overgeneralisation: Here's a great one: 'Women don't get promoted' – this is a real one that a client of mine once had. It's an overgeneralisation; it's a stereotype, but it's a common thinking trap that people fall into.

All or Nothing: If you ever hear yourself saying, 'I always blah blah blah' or 'I never blah blah blah', then it's a thinking trap because that's not true. Things are never *always*, and they are never *never*, either.

It's important to be aware that sometimes your thoughts are actually a clue to how you are feeling. Being able to label them brings them into existence and makes it much easier to identify them and point at them when you see them happening. This enables you to disconnect them from what is happening and look at a situation objectively.

As an example, you might think before a big important presentation: *'Why am I doing this? I'm not very good at these things. I'm not going to do this justice ...'* What might really be going on there is a sense of anxiety that's manifesting itself in your thoughts. Or maybe you're just frightened and feel fear. That's okay, you can actually talk yourself around from that; but just remember, fear is an emotional response to one predicted outcome, 'What if *this* happens?' Guilt and shame are about the past, worry and fear are about the future; futures that haven't happened yet. Often we get preoccupied worrying about the potential negative outcome instead of focusing our attention on another predicted outcome, the positive outcome. The positive outcome is what motivates and propels us forward, instead of holding us back, gripped by the fear of imagined 'what ifs?'.

As a result, it's important to pay attention to where our attention and thoughts are. We need to become aware of our own typical thinking traps. Everyone is different, but we tend to have preferences, which are often learned from our parents. If we can raise our awareness and think about our thinking (meta-thinking), we can tune into the voices in our head. Being aware of these 'thinking traps' is half the battle. Once you are aware of them, you can label them (e.g. 'I'm catastrophising again') and adjust for them. This gives you more control over the low-level narrative playing in the background of your mind.

The Committee

We aren't always aware of it, but most of us speak to ourselves through-out the day. Sometimes we don't even hear the words or sentences; we just get the feeling that comes with it (scorn, disappointment, frustra-tion, etc.).

Although the voice may be ours, it's often coming from a place that we don't recognise, and it can be really tough on us. You've probably heard of imposter syndrome, which is a classic voice among execs. It's the sense of questioning your achievements, a voice saying, 'How did I get here? Someone is going to find me out!', or a constant feeling that you're not quite as good as your job title suggests. I work with leaders all the way up and down the food chain, including many boards and CEOs, and I can tell you that imposter syndrome doesn't disappear the higher the rank of the exec. In fact, it often intensifies. The only way to make it go away is to put in the effort and challenge it head on.

'The Committee' is a great exercise to help you become aware of the different 'parts of you' and how you speak to yourself in a multi-tude of ways. The objective of this exercise is to hear the different ways you talk to yourself and then name them. By creating these 'charac-ters', you separate yourself from the voices ('It's not me, it's Sarcastic Susie'), thus taking some of their power away.

Part 1

- Think of the different situations when you tend to say something to yourself ('You're not good enough', 'I can't believe you just said that!', etc.).

- For each voice, decide if they're male or female (they might all be male, all female, or a mixture of both).

- Next, think of the tone or the emotion that comes from each voice. Maybe you get angry with yourself, or perhaps you speak to your-self sarcastically or in a ridiculing tone.

- For each voice think of a character's name that works with the description of the tone/emotion (e.g. Sarcastic Susie, Ridiculing Richard). Write their names below (Figure 8.2).

- Draw a face to represent the person – don't fall into the trap of telling yourself stories about whether you can or can't draw. It's not important; the exercise is what is important.

- Fill in the speech bubbles with what each character would typically say to you.

Now moving forward, when you speak to yourself in a negative way, try and pinpoint who in your Committee is talking (Figure 8.2).

Name them and give an explanation for why they are talking to you the way they are; for example, 'Oh, that's just Angry Anthony. He didn't get much sleep last night so he's very sensitive and quick to fly off the handle today. He just needs a good night's rest'. Or, 'That's

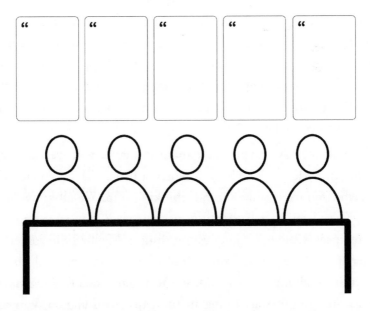

Figure 8.2   Recognising your Committee.

Judgemental Julie. She wants the very best for me, but no one can meet her ridiculously high standards'.

By doing this you are distancing yourself from the voice. It makes it much easier to ignore the voice or at least limit its power. Overall, this means the voice will have less control over you, and you can liberate yourself from its desire to self-sabotage!

Positive Thinking and Interpretation

As Zig Ziglar says, positive thinking will let you do everything better than negative thinking will. It's actually that simple. I want you to imagine the following scenario where you get a phone call from your boss:

'I know we're supposed to go away for a three-day business trip next week, but I'm sorry, something's come up, do you mind cancelling the hotel? We can chat tomorrow, but I have to go right now'.

What are you thinking after receiving that call? You could be thinking a million things. So, let's imagine you are on the verge of a promotion and this trip was an opportunity for you to 'shine' in front of your boss. What happens next? Take a second to actually write down what you think and feel as a result of that scenario, as well as what action you take.

Some time passes, you think about it, maybe you even talk about it with your friends. Maybe you worry a little. Maybe you're angry, or maybe you overthink; another thinking trap. We all know how it goes. We've been there so many times ourselves. You start imagining they're upset with you. You question things: 'Maybe I did something, or maybe they've had a conversation with someone and changed their minds about my capability'. You start second-guessing and mind-reading. You start filling in the gaps. In doing so, you make things up: 'Maybe they've decided to promote someone else They didn't give me an explanation, this is just disrespectful'. Everything gets bigger in your head.

Just pause and go back to the beginning. You received a phone call cancelling the business trip, and the other person said they would talk to you about it later. In the time between receiving the call and speaking to them, you've either not thought much more about it (which is rare) or you'll have worked yourself into a state. You'll be nervous (what's going to happen?) or upset (already sure the promotion has fallen through). Maybe you'll feel angry (how could they!?); maybe anxious (what will they say?). Maybe you've already decided you don't want the promotion anyway (self-protection).

All this time you've been creating what you think is happening. You go from fact to faction, to fiction, to fantasy; it's an arc. We do it all the time in our own storytelling, but it can be really dangerous. In that scenario, maybe when they ring you don't answer, or you answer saying, 'Yes?' (slightly impolitely or defensively). The other person responds to this emotion with, 'Oh, what's wrong with you?' You've made them defensive, and then the conversation unfolds, perhaps with more emotion than you would want.

When you start to second-guess people, you're mind-reading – an impossible feat. When you make a guess at what might be happening, often you unravel yourself and behave in a different way. Someone not returning a call, for example, could mean numerous things, such as that the person was really busy, distracted, something major happened – but often we tend to immediately attribute the reason to *us*.

This person who is cancelling the business trip might have just found out that the brand's travel budget has been cut in half, and they didn't have a chance to explain it to you because they were still fighting to get it reinstated. Maybe something personal is going on for them so they can't travel. There could be lots of reasons.

This can happen in also sorts of business situations: trying to get alignment on project plans, when trying to get budget approval or new resource to add to our team. If we fret about the outcome, we can often overlay meaning which doesn't exist. We see it happen a lot with the teams we work with; the dynamics within the team can be unhealthy because people are overlaying meaning onto one another's actions, raising suspicion and doubting people are taking the actions they should be to move a project forward. With one team we've worked with, it got so bad that in every meeting they were constantly questioning each other and asking for proof that certain meetings have happened with customers and that product testing is happening (can you send me photos?). When we overlay meaning where it does not exist, it can enhance our anxiety and lead us to actions which break trust within teams (like questioning people). That's why it's so important to not react in the moment, to not create stories around situations but to work with facts, because it's a slippery slope and can be the undoing of any good team.

In a situation like this, we have to try not to create the answers in our minds. There is no point in overthinking, because worrying will get you nowhere. It is the most wasted past-time I've ever experienced. All it does is work you up into a state. It's a very personal emotion, it's quite exhausting and it's really just not that helpful.

When a situation happens, you will, of course, find yourself second-guessing, but you need to stop yourself if you want to have an easier life, and if you want to enter the conversation from a neutral place instead of already being in a 'hot state', charged, already angry, or already disappointed. If you work within a team and in your meetings you hear people say, 'Well, I think, they think …' That's an immediate red flag. As you learn to navigate this for yourself, it's important that you also teach the team that you work within (or lead) how to avoid the pitfalls of the mind. Always make sure you take action on data, not hidden assumptions. When you realise you don't have enough data, go get some, don't make it up!

> A wise man knows you only have one enemy, yourself. This enemy, it's difficult to ignore and it's full of cunning.
>
> – *Anon.*

We self-sabotage all the time without ever recognising it. I often say to people:

'If we were to take what we say to ourselves out of our head and say it to somebody else, they'd punch us in the face'.

We can be so tough on ourselves. Even the best of us can automatically default to negative thinking. Why is that? The answer is the negativity bias. We are pre-programmed to pay more attention to the negative things in life than the positive things in life. Psychologist Daniel Kahneman, in *Thinking, Fast and Slow*, talks about how 'the brains of humans and other animals contain a mechanism that is designed to give priority to bad news. By shaving a few hundredths of a second from the time needed to detect a predator, this circuit improves the animal's odds of living long enough to reproduce'.[1]

Paying more attention to the negative than to the positive is built into us because it's negative things that save our lives. Remember, in Chapter 4 I talked about uncertainty? It's the same thing. When we're uncertain we hesitate, and when we hesitate, we die. It's more important to pay attention to the negative thoughts than to the positive thoughts because they keep us alive, but many of those survival threats aren't with us any more.

In the next chapter, I'll explain what's happening in your mind with a little bit of neurology. This will also demonstrate how you can overcome this pre-programming.

---

[1] Kahneman, D. (2011) *Thinking, Fast and Slow*, New York, NY: Farrar, Straus and Giroux.

27 years ago I read the book "The 7 Habits of Highly Effective People" and the one habit that really stuck with me was "sharpening the saw", which is about taking care of yourself. It was much more in the infant phases back then, but Stephen Covey was already thinking about the modern workplace and the skillset of future leaders. I actually see that it's becoming more and more important today and certainly over the last five years, because the world is ever changing and certainly during COVID that makes things more uncertain and more difficult for employees to deal with. We all need to be working on enhancing our mental fitness so we are fighting fit for the future that's ahead of us.

– Nathalie Slechte, Chief HR Officer, JDE

9 Fear Response and Neuroplasticity

Let me share a little bit of neurology to help bring this to life.

There's a part of the brain that sits above the brainstem, called the amygdala. It has many functions, but its main function is the fight, flight, or freeze function. The amygdala is part of the reptilian brain, which is how we refer to the part that's been there since the beginning of evolution. It's this part that helps us to stay alive. It's our fear centre. When we face a threat, our amygdala shoots off a message to our prefrontal cortex.

Our prefrontal cortex is right at the front of the brain. This is what differentiates us from other mammals in the animal kingdom, because they don't have a prefrontal cortex. Its role is logic and reasoning. Imagine that the amygdala shoots off a message saying, 'You're in danger, you're in danger, you need to run or freeze'. The prefrontal cortex then assesses the situation and sends a message back to the amygdala saying, 'Shh, it's okay, this is under control, we've got this. You're not going to die. There's no real threat here, it's just a text message from your boss saying, "Where are you?" They probably want a cappuccino'.

There's another part of the brain called the nucleus accumbens, which is your pleasure centre. So, when you're eating chocolate, for example, it might send a message to the prefrontal cortex saying, 'Mm, this is good, I want more'.

The prefrontal cortex might send a message back saying, 'No, you've had too much, you've had enough, calm down'. What I'm trying to demonstrate is how important the role of the prefrontal cortex is, particularly in relation to those neural pathways. Until recently, we believed that the brain stopped changing at about the age of 12, at which point your neural pathways were your neural pathways for life. More recently, in the last 10 years, we have found evidence to support the fact that we can continue to change our brain as we get older.

Neural-elasticity, or neuroplasticity, really is just that; it's about the brain being elastic or plastic: it can change, be moulded, develop, and grow (Figure 9.1). That is amazing news for us, because it means that we can grow and change our neural pathways. Just as we exercise

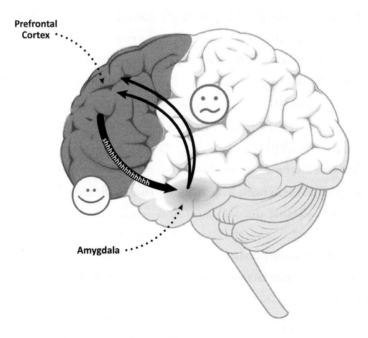

Figure 9.1   Neuroplasticity explained.

our muscles in the gym, we need to exercise the neural pathways in our minds.

Research[1] conducted by neurobiologist Richard Davidson discovered there were differences between the neural pathways in the brains of optimistic people and pessimistic people.

The positive people had really strong neural pathways from the prefrontal cortex back to their amygdala, the part that self-soothes and says, 'Shh, you're okay, don't overreact'. Negative and pessimistic people had really strong neural pathways from their amygdala to their prefrontal cortex, which is the survival mechanism, but the pathway back to the self-soothing part was really weak and, in some cases, almost non-existent.

What they discovered is that it's possible to strengthen the neural pathway from the prefrontal cortex back to the amygdala through mindful meditation, self-talk, and practice (the exercises in this book are ideal for enhancing those neural pathways, if utilised regularly).

If you meditate for 20 minutes a day, every day, for up to four weeks, it changes the neural pathways in your mind. It makes a positive connection stronger, and it makes you better equipped to deal with shocks, situations, tragedies, surprises, setbacks, and challenges. It helps you reset yourself, and that's fantastic news, there's hope for us all! These are things you can apply in your life so that you can continue to change, grow, and evolve.

Elaine Fox, the cognitive psychologist, has written a book, *Sunny Brain, Rainy Brain*. I highly recommend reading it if you'd like to learn a bit more about neuroplasticity. In this book, she explains that the brain's circuits that underpin our pessimistic and our optimistic brain are actually the most plastic within the human brain. That's really good news for us. She uses the analogy of the brain's circuits being like water moving through sand. Think about how, when the tide goes out, a

---

[1] Davidson, R. J. and McEwen, B. S. (2012, April 15) 'Social Influences on Neuroplasticity: Stress and Interventions to Promote Well-Being', *Nature Neuroscience*, 15 (5): 689–695.

small stream can be left in the sand where the water has created a pathway. As more water flows along this pathway back towards the sea, it becomes wider and deeper.

That's exactly how our neural pathways work as well. So, if you have a tendency to think negatively, that pathway gets thicker and thicker and thicker, and it flows really naturally. It becomes the default pathway in your thinking. The same is also true of positive thinking. Changing these pathways isn't easy and takes effort, but the point is that you *can* change them.

If you need to change the pathway that the water's flowing down, you need to practise 'self-soothing', which is the ability to calm the mind when it spirals. We don't want you to do this just for the sake of it, but because, as I mentioned earlier, our brain hasn't had a hardware update for millennia. It still acts as though we have predators and that our survival is under daily threat. Therefore, we need to offset this neural wiring (from the amygdala to the pre-frontal cortex) by strengthening the pathway from the pre-frontal cortex back to the amygdala by practising the techniques in this book. Why should you do it? Because you're actually changing the wiring of your brain. You're changing your neural pathways; and the more you practise, the easier it will become, until it's your natural way of being. I share much more detail on the neuroscience behind this in the stress and performance Chapter 16 towards the end of the book. You can skip ahead if, like me, you're into the science. Just don't forget to come back!

How Heavy Is Your Glass?

In my Mental Fitness workshops, I include a number of simple yet powerful demonstrations. One of the simplest exercises is holding up a glass of water and asking people to guess how heavy it is. People shout out numbers. Sometimes one bright spark says, 'It depends', or they make a reference to optimism or pessimism (glass half full/empty).

The point I'm making with this demonstration is that it doesn't matter how heavy it is, what matters is how long I hold it.

The longer I hold on to it, the heavier it becomes, and the more my arm aches. The more pain I feel, the more focus it steals from me. The more attention it has, the more I complain about it, and the more frustrating it is. It becomes more and more and more difficult to hold as it becomes heavier and heavier and heavier, even though its weight hasn't changed. The issue is that I am holding on to it.

This is exactly how you should think about your negative thoughts and the stories you tell yourself: *I'm not good enough, I don't deserve it, I'm too old, too young, too fat, too thin, I'm not ready, not yet …* whatever they might be. This is how your team should think about those unhelpful thoughts keeping you from your goals – 'We'll never reach this years' target', 'How can we increase penetration when it's already at 80%!' Whatever thoughts are holding you back, just like this glass of water, the more you hold on to them, the more distraction and discomfort they will bring. The solution is quite simple: to release yourself and your teams, you need to put down that glass of water; you need to let go of those thoughts that are contaminating your mind and your mental fitness.

Our ways of thinking are habitual. To change them takes effort, just like trying to break any habit. To quote Mark Manson, 'You can't grow muscle without challenging it with greater weight. You can't build emotional resilience without forging through hardship. You can't build a better mind without challenging your own beliefs and assumptions'. That's exactly what we're going to work on: tuning into the thoughts in your mind and those of your team.

People often say to me, 'Oh, I don't know why I always think this way. I want to stop but I just can't'. Well, most likely, you just don't know how to. Being told to think positively really isn't helpful. I'm going to give you strategies, tools, techniques, and exercises to help break that apart for you. Changing your habits and your habitual ways of thinking requires a commitment and effort from you. If you're up for it, I'm going to show you exactly how to do that. These are tools for you, but you can also use them with your teams and the people you care about to help them reframe some of their more limiting thinking patterns.

We need to reposition mental health conversations away from just communicating and keeping strategies, to helping people build thriving strategies. Given that the environment that people are going to be working in is going to be a tougher one, how are you going to recruit people to thrive in that environment? We need to be thinking differently, not about stopping ill health but enhancing mental fitness to be ready for the future of work.

— *Head of Wellbeing, Global Financial Services*

Humans are capable of creating awesome stuff when we come together. And we will only accept or give help if we trust each other. What is trust? It's a feeling; it's a thought. So, interestingly one of the most important currencies of organisational behaviour – of people coming together to do wildly amazing things is trust, which is purely a thought and a feeling.

— *Matthew McCarthy, CEO, Ben & Jerry's*

Part Four
Limiting and Empowering Beliefs

This part goes a layer deeper than thinking and will help you to look at the rules you have made up for your life, often unknowingly. The aim here is to bring the areas where you may have already 'predetermined your fate' into your consciousness. These areas can relate to your capability, your potential in the future, and your judgement on yourself and others.

We all have both empowering and limiting beliefs. Unfortunately though, we tend to have more limiting beliefs than empowering ones, and it's the limiting beliefs that hold us back and stop us from showing up in our truest form in life. They prevent us from being brave and courageous.

Limiting beliefs manifest as that little voice in your head that tells you 'you're not good enough'; 'not yet'; 'it's not meant for you'; 'it's too big a risk'. We want to acknowledge that voice but not give it all-out power – because it is the voice of your insecurities speaking, or someone else's judgement of your capabilities. Just as you wouldn't constantly react to your over-anxious neighbour down the road every time you hear them, the same is true of your limiting beliefs.

The first step is to discover which limiting beliefs exist in your life. Then seek to understand where they come from and what they are costing you in your life. Next, you need to challenge and reframe them. This part of the book will give you the practical know-how to first be able to recognise your limiting beliefs and then to reframe a definitive 'rule' into a statement that opens up new possibilities. When you start to do this and see what it releases in you, it can become addictive because it frees up so many more opportunities and possibilities in your life.

Just as individuals have limiting beliefs, so too can teams. More often than not, when a team is not making a shared goal happen, it's because there is a collective belief holding them back – whether that's because they just don't think the goal is possible or something else. Either way, these collective beliefs show up as resistance within the team. Uncovering them allows you to talk about them and prepare an action plan against them. In this section, I'll also share how you can identify team beliefs and what to do about them when you find them.

10 The 'Rules' We Should Be Breaking

You may have heard the term *limiting beliefs* before. When we talk about beliefs in general, it can take people's minds to religion, politics, and so on. But really what we are referring to are the 'rules' we have made up about our life, our capabilities, what is possible, what isn't possible, and so on.

Each one of us holds a range of beliefs or judgements about ourselves and the world, which we assume to be true, even if there's no evidence to support them (hence the term 'rules'). Some of these beliefs are useful to us, but most can be harmful for our performance. They're the self-inflicted rules that we've created for ourselves, usually showing up as generalisations and sweeping statements about our abilities. These can also be reinforced over time and through experience.

They usually get developed during our formative years or when we try new things. We can also inherit belief systems from our parents, teachers, bosses, teammates, and anyone who has a significant role in our lives. Of course, at a macro level, politics, culture, and religion also play a role in instilling certain beliefs in us.

The issue many of us face is that, most of the time, we don't even know these beliefs are there.

Because we start to adopt many beliefs early in life, they can be so deeply rooted in our minds that we don't even notice them. They exist in the background of our minds, colouring our perception and influencing our thoughts and behaviour. Even if you don't know they're there, they will be limiting the possibilities and opportunities in your life.

> Whether you believe you can or you believe you can't, you're probably right.
>
> – *Henry Ford*

The beliefs we created when we were younger tend to have quite a strong hold on us and are difficult to remove; difficult, but not impossible. The thing about beliefs is that they don't represent who we are, they represent who we have learned to be. Young children don't go around saying, 'I mustn't do this, I shouldn't do that, I'm not good enough, I'm not ready'; they run around shouting, 'Me, me, me'. No matter what we are doing, my three-year-old will always shout, 'Me turn, me turn', even if it's driving a car!

We didn't have limitations when we were young, we pushed ourselves, we did things even though we didn't know how; we tried things anyway. That's how we learned and grew. Not knowing or not being able wasn't a reason 'not to'. Indeed, it's pretty standard when you're two that you don't know much, and it doesn't matter.

Along the way we lose the gung-ho attitude, the experimental approach to life, the courage to say 'me next'. We often lose it because of small incidents, long forgotten. A flippant remark from a relative, a teacher, a parent, a neighbour who said, 'Oh no, not you, because … ' – you can fill in the blank. We all have one, we all have many. We picked up these 'rules', these beliefs, which now have us playing small, somewhere along the way.

Slowly but surely, each of these beliefs has piled up, taking the colour and courage from our personalities, the self-belief from our arms that used to shoot up as we said, 'Me next, my turn'. But this doesn't have to be the end of the story. If we want agile teams and adaptable people, willing to take risks and innovate for the future, we all need to learn how to rewrite our scripts, if we're willing. The first step is to find the script.

We need to become aware of what 'rules' we have created about our capabilities, but beliefs are tricky little things because we are so used to living with them we often just take them as facts. They tend to slip into conversation unnoticed and therefore unchallenged. For example, *'I'm not a natural at languages'* or *'I'm nervous when I'm in meetings with senior people'.* If a friend or colleague said this to you, you would most likely nod in understanding, maybe even agreement, or continue the conversation without noticing that this is a belief masquerading as a fact.

The truth is we have all sorts of beliefs, but they usually fall into two categories: empowering or limiting. As you can guess, the empowering ones are the good ones! They motivate you and propel you forward. They might include beliefs like:

'I love solving problems'.

'I'm great at thinking on my feet'.

'Speaking in front of an audience energises me', etc.

We don't want to touch the empowering ones. It's the limiting ones that we want to flush out and challenge, because they influence what we do, how we conduct ourselves, and the decisions we make, in a way that usually holds us back.

Beliefs are generalisations that tend to be sweeping and all-encompassing, and they shape our map of reality. The good news is that it's possible for our beliefs and also our values to change over time, but they will only change if they are challenged. They can be challenged by a big life event or, with a little bit of effort, we can challenge them consciously.

Why Do We Form Limiting Beliefs?

The answer is that they actually simplify our lives in many ways. Their existence means we don't have to consciously assess every situation; we have shortcuts as to what *is* and what *is not* possible, or as to what *is* a good course of action and what *is not*. This creates efficiencies in the mind, and our brain loves efficiency as it frees up cognitive processing space for more important matters like focusing on threats, problem solving, etc.

For example, imagine that when you were four or five you put your hand on a hot stove and you got burnt. It only really takes that to happen once for you to learn the rule that 'hot stoves are dangerous' and for you to never do it again.

These beliefs are not just for learning how to protect ourselves. The efficiencies are everywhere. Can you imagine if, every time you had to make a coffee, you had to sit down and consider how you liked your coffee? Should you have instant or filter, add sugar or not, with dairy milk or soya? How much time and cognitive resource would that take? And then having to do it two to three times a day!

Our brain wants to free itself up for the new and important stuff, so it's always creating shortcuts and high-level rules that it can apply automatically. This is where habits come from, as well as stereotypes and, of course, beliefs. In principle they are designed to simplify our lives (although often they complicate them!).

Beliefs are also designed for us to learn from past experiences, so we don't repeat mistakes. This is the same reason why we sometimes find ourselves buying into generalisations and stereotypes – simply because it's easy and neurologically efficient. But it's not always helpful, nor is it usually positive (because we are wired for survival and will prioritise creating rules about potential threats over everything else).

That's why it's essential for us all to examine the rules we've made up for ourselves and ask ourselves, 'Is this helpful? Is this positive?' If it's neither, then we need to challenge the rules and remove them from our lives.

Although beliefs can be helpful when they are protecting us, the problem occurs when we learn 'rules' that aren't true; in this case, they aren't protecting us or helping us, but instead are holding us back. It's important, therefore, to sift through all of the beliefs we have, work out what's serving us and what isn't, and then challenge and 'reframe' those beliefs that are holding us back.

Our beliefs and our perceptions combined inspire us to act or stop us from acting. They are subconsciously guiding our decisions in life.

Remember the mind-body connection triangle? Our beliefs, values, and experiences influence each part (thinking, feeling, acting) and give us our world view.

Let's bring that to life through an example. I want you to imagine you are about to give a presentation to, let's say, 20–30 people. You walk into the room thinking, *'I'm terrible at presentations. I'm not good with an audience'*. That's your belief, right? I know you think it might be a fact, but it's not. It's a belief, a rule that you've made up about your own capability.

Even though you are nervous, you start the presentation, and you give it your best effort. From the corner of your eye you see someone in the front row yawn. The yawn is meaningless – but because of your belief that you're terrible at presentations, you overlay meaning.

You think to yourself, *'Oh no! He's bored, that's because I'm boring. He thinks this presentation is terrible. I knew I was going to be bad because I'm not good at presentations. Why did I say yes to this? I should never say yes again!'*

Of course, then you have an emotional response to your thoughts. After thinking, you feel nervous and anxious. This affects your physiology and subsequently your behaviour. Perhaps your palms get sweaty, your voice shakes, you stop making eye contact. You speed up through the charts. You're not engaging with the audience; you just want it to be over.

The next time you look up, people in the audience are looking back at you a little strangely (because they're responding to you suddenly speeding up, not making eye contact, and being a bit nervous).

You take this as further confirmation that this is awful and that you are terrible. You move even more quickly, determined to get this over with so you can leave, and you tell yourself, *'Never put yourself in that situation again because you are awful at presentations!'*

Or, you walk into the room thinking, *'This is going to be great, I love this topic and I'm really excited to finally get to share my point of view and hear other people's points of view'* – that's an example of an empowering belief.

The same thing happens: someone in the front row yawns. You either don't notice, you ignore it, or you think to yourself, *'Hmm maybe it's a bit warm in here actually, I'll see if I can get the aircon on'*, or you think, *'I bet he's been working really hard, and I know he's got a heavy workload, but he was so interested in this topic he came to listen anyway'*. And you continue as usual.

Exactly the same thing happened.

The difference was what you *thought* in the first place about your own capabilities (whether you had a limiting belief or an empowering one), and the meaning you decided to overlay onto the yawn and how that subsequently affected your thoughts, feelings, and behaviours for the good and for the bad.

Here's the thing. We add meaning to things all the time, so why not add the useful meaning?! The helpful stories and thoughts that will encourage us to perform in the moment rather than undo ourselves and make us want to run out of the room!

We spend so much time working on external characteristics, how we present, the arguments we make on businesses cases, our ability to influence, come up with good marketing ideas, and so on. If we only put a fraction of that effort into mastering our inner game, we'd all be laughing. You see, if we're not doing the inner work, understanding where our insecurities lie, what beliefs are holding us back, how to enhance our resilience to setbacks, and so on, then we don't have a chance in the outer game. We've got to be playing *for* ourselves, not *against* ourselves. The reality is we are going to meet many people in our lives and careers who will be critical, hold us back, and tell us that we're not ready and not good enough. *We* should *not* be one of them! That is as true for individuals as it is for teams.

Beliefs and Teams

Many of the teams that come to us want to sharpen their ways of working, collaborate better, increase productivity, and so on. They are all great goals, but the route to achieving them is by accessing our inner resources and enhancing our mental fitness. We can't collaborate efficiently if we haven't connected at a meaningful level, by which I mean properly understanding each other's (and our own) drivers, motivators, values, strengths and weaknesses, and so on. It's this clarity, and vulnerability, that unites teams towards a shared goal. No matter what objectives we are working towards when running sessions with leaders or their teams, we *always* spend time understanding the individuals who make up that team – from their perception of the challenge, to their thinking surrounding their vision, from their shared beliefs (the helpful and the unhelpful) to their individual and shared values. Without doing this deeper work, we're always just working at surface level.

No matter what it is you are trying to achieve in life or in business, if you find yourself not achieving it or always facing obstacles, there will be two reasons why. The first is that it's not really what you or your team want. Maybe it's what your boss, the company, or shareholders want, but you, as a team, don't believe it's aligned or right for your brand or business function. Then all attempts to move forward are futile. That's true of you own personal goals. If you're not making progress it's because there's a good chance that it's not what you want but what your partner wants or what you think society expects from you. You're not making it happen, because deep down you're not connected to the goal. In business you must always ensure that the people working in your team want to be there and believe in the overall vision or goal. If they don't, you'll experience a hidden 'drag' in the system.

The second reason, if it's not the first, will simply be that you or your team don't believe the goal is achievable. When you talk about it with your friends or colleagues, it may sound like it really is what you want, but I can guarantee you, if you're not making it happen, it's because deep down there is something working against you: a belief you have that's holding you back. It may be one of the foundational beliefs many of us have:

- 'I'm not good enough to achieve this'.
- 'We're not ready'.
- 'It's too big or unrealistic'.
- 'I can't do this because of X, Y, Z'.

Or a more specific belief; below are some examples from clients who struggled to meet their personal goals:

- 'Only multimillionaires get to retire in their fifties'.
- 'To live in another country, you need to be X, Y, Z and I'm not those'.
- 'To set up your own business you have to have an extremely unique idea that no one has ever done before'.
- 'Only men get promoted to the board. As a female, I would have to work three times harder and I don't have the energy for that'.

In business, I've run many a workshop on unlocking future growth, which usually always involves creating a clear vision for the future; often there's a buzz in the room as people brainstorm and thrash it out. But sometimes, once the vision is clear the room can split. We'll have some people pumped up and excited, and others lurking in the background and not saying much – it usually leads to a strange energy in the room. When I pick up on this I always dig deeper. If something feels odd, it's usually because there's some unspoken resistance in the room. The best way to do this is to turn the vision or goal on its head, go to the flipchart with pen poised and ask everyone to shout out as many reasons as possible for why this vision or goal is *never* going to happen. I tell people, 'I just want you to role-play' (that's just an easy way of giving them permission to tell us their innermost worries without committing career suicide). Every time we get a list of things, the real obstacles usually pop out just at the end (which is why it's good to be exhaustive). Then we get to look at the board and ask 'which of these are real threats we should be addressing?' You can narrow them down to the 3–5 real ones which have potential to cause you trouble later down the line. Then we focus on coming up with a plan for pre-empting them before they become visible. I can tell you it saves months of setbacks and drag in the system to do this one exercise. It's also quite cathartic for the team because they get to 'confess' to all their concerns. The issues also largely get addressed in the room, by other people, and if they can't they become part of the risk mitigation list with an action plan beside each one. Before going 90 miles an hour behind any business objectives, always make sure you flush out the limiting beliefs in the room first.

You may not be aware that beliefs like this are lurking around in your mind (or that of your teams), or maybe they only come up when you're in deep conversations about the topic. If you're working with a coach, they will be spotted quite quickly and presented to you, and they'll usually ask you if you want to challenge them. But if you're working alone, you'll need to learn how to notice your own limiting beliefs by yourself. The rest of this chapter helps with that, but more importantly will teach you how to challenge limiting beliefs as well.

Spotting Limiting Beliefs

Our language often gives away our limiting beliefs. Therefore, exploring our language is a good place to start when you're learning how to spot limiting beliefs. To help you easily identify them, we'll give examples of typical beliefs I've come across over my years of coaching (see Figure 10.1). I'll also share some of my own limiting beliefs.

The language we use are clues and are the indicators that we have limiting beliefs, but they can also be well disguised, such as *'Oh, I won't go for that promotion because I'm not ready, I've still got more to learn here'*. This is where we are convincing ourselves that things are okay, often because we are afraid to move forward or because moving forward will take too much effort or represents too much of a risk. Be careful of the beliefs that are masquerading as 'fair arguments'.

I talked about 'mind chatter' in the chapter about thinking. Our mind chatter is often full of limiting beliefs. To find beliefs in our mind

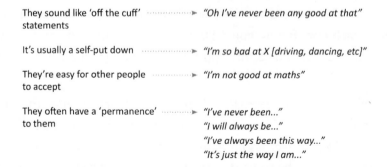

Figure 10.1   How to spot a limiting belief.

chatter, we just need to tune into it and listen for the above clues to pull out what the beliefs are.

The opening words that normally hint at your limiting beliefs are, 'Life is …' followed by a big sweeping statement; conclusive statements like, 'I am not good at this', or, 'I'm the type of person who …'

We can also recognise our limiting beliefs in our feelings. Imagine you're facing a big issue at the moment. Maybe you feel anxious, angry, or hopeless. If you stay with the emotion and just dig underneath the surface, you'll be able to find a belief behind it.

Let's take, for example, anxiety. Maybe behind anxiety is, 'What will my colleagues think of me?' It's sometimes a fear of judgement. Behind anger could be, 'Life in business just isn't fair', or, 'People just aren't good to me'.

Perhaps underneath hopelessness might be:

- 'Oh, I'm just not strong enough to deal with this'.
- 'I'm not good enough'.
- 'I'm not smart enough to figure this out'.
- 'I've never been good with numbers'.

Relationship beliefs are also quite common because they are usually quite emotionally charged, and we tend to subconsciously learn a rule from them. If you have a bad experience with a boss, you might have learned, 'I'm not good enough', or, 'I don't deserve a promotion'. Or you might relate working relationships to suffering and therefore have learned the rule that 'work relationships are difficult'. That's quite a common one. Or maybe you were overlooked for promotion, and you've decided, 'All bosses are too demanding'.

In the spirit of sharing, I am going to share with you some of my old limiting beliefs. Thankfully, I have spent considerable time reframing and challenging them so now they've got no hold over me, but perhaps you might identify with them. I used to have:

- 'I'm not good at reading maps'.
- 'I'm not a natural at languages'.
- 'I'm not good with numbers'.
- 'I need a PhD in order to be credible enough to write a book'.

I'm sure you can identify with one or two of those. At first glance, they don't even seem like a big issue. Indeed, some of your limiting beliefs won't be costing you that much. However, some will be, and without exploring them you won't realise how much.

For example, *'I'm not good with numbers'* doesn't seem like a big deal. I remember exactly when I adopted this belief. I was 14, our classroom maths teacher was walking the room throwing back (that was his style) marked tests. Mine landed abruptly on my desk, 67% in big red pen with a circle around it. I actually thought 67% was a pretty good mark to be honest, but because it was in red pen, as well as being thrown at me without a word or even eye contact, this led me to believe the mark was bad and something to be ashamed of. A number of other smaller 'confirmations' solidified the belief that I was bad at maths and terrible at anything to do with numbers.

This made me avoid mental arithmetic in front of people. I didn't want to work out the bill when eating with friends and so on. Still no big deal, right? Interestingly, for most of my adult life, friends and colleagues regularly told me I should have my own business (for various different reasons), but the thought of it petrified me. Why? Because I thought business meant numbers and if I wasn't any good with numbers, I wouldn't be able to have a business.

That's when you start to see how a small, seemingly harmless belief can have a disproportionate impact on your life. What makes it more complicated is, being human, I had come up with lots of rational and logical reasons why I didn't *want* my own business (in truth I did, but I had too much fear around the numbers issue) – these rational reasons were there to protect me, to protect my dignity, pride, and sense of self. However, the logical reasons were masking the true emotional reason (fear), which in turn was driven by my 'harmless' beliefs around maths/numbers/business capability.

All of this was happening subconsciously. I wasn't aware of this complex web of thoughts, beliefs, and emotions. I fully believed myself (see how tricky it is?!) that I didn't want a business. It wasn't until I was working with a coach (I was working on something else entirely) that the belief popped up. Even then I dismissed it: 'So what, no big deal about numbers, calculators exist!' It was when the coach helped me unpack it that I could see all of the areas in my life where this limiting belief was holding me back and 'costing' me. That was when I personally realised the power of seemingly 'harmless thoughts'.

Many of the first beliefs I uncovered I did so accidentally, leading to a wider journey of 'conscious' discovery which continues to this day (yes, there are always more of them to deal with!). What about you? Have you found any of yours?

Well, now is the perfect opportunity. I encourage you to get a pen and paper and write a list of the ones that might come up for you about:

- Your capability
- Your relationship to 'success'
- Your attitude to money
- Your beliefs about the future

Below I've given you some common 'general' limiting beliefs, to help you identify some of yours.

The 'Not Enoughs'

- I'm not good enough.
- I'm not smart enough.
- I'm not talented enough.
- I'm not experienced enough.
- I don't fit in enough.

The 'Too Much' or 'Too Littles'

It's not meant for you because ...

- I'm too old/young.
- I'm too tall/short.
- I'm too ugly/pretty.
- I'm too different.

The 'White Rabbits' (all about time)

- It's not my time.
- It's too late.
- It's too early.
- I'm not ready.

The 'Undeserveds'

- I don't deserve it.
- I haven't worked hard enough yet.
- It's for people who are smarter/more talented than me.
- It's not for people like me.

You might also have specific beliefs, for example, about your career, your employer, your fitness, your appearance, and so on:

- I'm too young/old to get promoted.
- You need to work around the clock, work evenings and weekends to get noticed in work.
- I don't have the right experience to make it.
- To be a senior leader here, you need to be X, Y, Z.
- It's impossible to have a successful career and be a mum.
- You have to be cut-throat to make it to the top.
- I'm no good at office politics, so I'll never get anywhere.

I bet you've heard people say some of these. I know I have; maybe *you've* even said them.

Maybe you're sitting there thinking, but these are all *true*.

That's the trick. Limiting beliefs sound plausible, which is why we agree with our friends and colleagues instead of challenging their thinking.

The problem is, whether they're true or not doesn't even matter. The moment we accept a thought like one of the above, it limits our lives. Why? Because we hold ourselves back on the assumption that it's true. We make different decisions because of it.

If you carry any of these beliefs, you will not even attempt to go for a promotion, you will not try and be successful, you will not try to grow – because you're defeated before you start.

Let's bring that to life with one last specific example from the world of sports, more specifically, golf. Imagine it's the night before a big championship, and a golfer is staying at a hotel on the grounds where the competition will take place. One of his limiting beliefs is,

'I'm off my game when it rains' and another one is, 'My mental game is weak'.

The next morning he wakes up, pulls back the curtains, and it's raining. What do you think that does for him? How do you think that affects his thinking? His feelings? And subsequently his performance?

Sportspeople actually know the importance of the mental game, and the rest of us really are just catching up. They have coaches for their sport and they have coaches for their mental game. But they can still fall into unhelpful thinking traps and belief systems. We need to put as much effort into our 'mental game' as sportspeople do.

Can you imagine a sportsperson, ahead of a big day, sitting up working late on their computer, getting up and running out of the door with just a coffee in their belly, skipping breakfast? Absolutely not. In a business context, you might do this so you can write some last-minute PowerPoint charts; you're worrying and becoming anxious because, 'You're not good at public speaking'. This is your preparation before standing up in front of a senior audience to 'perform'. Would you expect to be at your best in that situation? Absolutely not, but we do it all the time.

We need to be aware of what's going on inside ourselves. We need to tune into our inner game so that we can consciously manage it, because if we don't, our mind runs away with itself.

As soon as we think an unhelpful thought or remind ourselves of a limiting belief, it'll affect how we feel, which will affect how we perform.

This is not just true for individuals but also for teams and groups of people. We can collectively believe in possibility or impossibility. If a brand team subconsciously believes that they will never be number one in a key market, that is exactly what will happen. Because of that collective (often unsaid) belief, they will make slightly different (often less brave) decisions. It's the mindset difference between trying to hold on to market share (not lose against competitors/local brands) versus gaining market share and growing. A small shift in thinking can lead to big results.

The team that collectively believes it's possible to be number one will take greater risks, be more responsive to market changes, and overall have a 'winning mindset'.

This is also true for general beliefs that affect teams. For instance, the belief, 'We are better together' helps create and instil effective collaboration behaviours. The issue with teams is that they don't always talk about their collective beliefs. If they aren't discussed, then they aren't seen. If they aren't seen, they can't be challenged.

When I work with leadership teams and their wider teams, I spend time upfront unpacking the beliefs they have, because these beliefs are where unhelpful and sometimes harmful behaviours can stem from.

For example, I once worked with a team in the ice cream category, and I knew going in that they weren't great at collaborating. It would have been easy then to think the solution was training or practice in new collaboration techniques. However, they had been receiving training in agile methods and collaboration tools for the last 12 months. Although this can sometimes work, often the answer isn't always the obvious solution (e.g. collaboration training). This goes back to what I was saying right at the beginning of the book: we often spend too much time in business solving the wrong problems.

In the diagnosis stage of our work together, I realised that collaboration was a *symptom*; it wasn't the problem, there was a bigger underlying issue – a lack of trust. The trust issue had a number of contributing factors to it which we had to unpack. These factors included past issues (and wounds), ego-centred personalities, overwork, and feeling overwhelmed. However, the main factor was an overriding belief that *'there is no time to work with others; working with other people just slows things up, I need to keep my head down and get the job done by myself'*.

Interestingly, although most of the team had this attitude, it was most prevalent among the longest-serving team members. My job was then to prove that this was a shared unconscious belief, and that it wasn't true. I did this by using demonstrations, shared exercises, some education, and generally shaking up their behaviours. I also taught the team some easy and fast ways to get inputs from others (without taking time); I showed them how to 'reframe problems' and how to brainstorm in under 15 minutes, among other techniques. All these exercises were to disprove that limiting belief.

I then continued to work with the team for a further six months, and, slowly but surely, trust levels increased, people began to communicate more, and they began to reach out to others. Initially they only reached out for early inputs and ideas, but eventually this evolved to full collaboration on projects. It took time, but we got there. I wouldn't have got anywhere, however, if I had just trained them to use collaboration tools. That's the importance of separating symptoms from causes.

I first had to show them the shared limiting belief and then work at disproving it (removing the obstacle). Only then was I able to leverage collaboration techniques, because now they were willing and open to collaboration.

Whether it's individual limiting beliefs or collective limiting beliefs, we need to first identify these beliefs and then challenge them through reframing. Later I'll share one of my techniques to reframe. Right now, I want to explain *why* we should reframe limiting beliefs (besides the obvious reasons).

Why Reframing Beliefs Matters Neurologically

We've long been told to think positively, to try not to focus on the negative and, for some, to even repeat positive affirmations. But most people don't explain *why* this matters. Knowing the neurological and psychological reasoning behind such advice has been the biggest motivating factor for me to strive to master my thinking and my emotions (or at least not be 'victim' to them). It's this information that shifted me into powerful behaviour change in my personal and professional life. I'm hoping it will shift you and your teams as well. Let me tell you about the Reticular Activating System (Figure 10.2).

The Reticular Activating System (RAS) is a part of the brain that's responsible for regulating several brain functions, such as wakefulness and sleep cycles. It also influences where we focus our attention. We're bombarded by sensory information all the time – it's difficult to say exactly, but research sources indicate that we attend to between 10 and 1000 million bits of data per second at an unconscious level. For the sake of simplicity, we can at least say the power of the unconscious mind is much faster than that of our conscious mind.

We can't consciously 'attend' to millions of bits of information at once. We can only attend to around 40 bits of data each second.

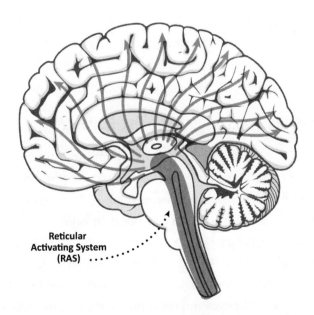

Figure 10.2 The Reticular Activating System (RAS).

As such, we need filtering systems to help us quickly and easily know what to focus on.

The RAS, in part, acts as this filter and determines what is raised from our subconscious to our conscious attention levels. It will always prioritise anything novel or strange (as this could be a threat to our survival), anything personal (e.g. our name) as it's more likely to be relevant, and anything else we tell it is important – in other words, the things that we're currently focusing on (irrespective of whether they are good or bad!). It can therefore reinforce our thinking by being selective about what we pay attention to.

We've all experienced the RAS in action. Remember the last time you were considering buying a car? Suddenly, that particular model (maybe even in your chosen colour) becomes the only car you see on the road. There's one parked beside you at the supermarket; one passes you on the motorway; there's an advert for it on TV. It must be a sign! No – it's your RAS. You've told yourself this specific car is important. All the other car models and colours are still on the road; your brain is just filtering them out.

Our thoughts and our beliefs 'program' our RAS. The more we say something to ourselves, the more important it is considered to be.

How Does Our Focus Reinforce Our Beliefs?

Our RAS can work for or against us by filtering out any information that contradicts our beliefs. If our beliefs are positive, then we're only aware of evidence that reinforces them (this is also known as the confirmation bias). Similarly, for our negative beliefs, we will only see the evidence that supports them, the evidence that makes us believe they're true. The reality is there is usually evidence for everything, it just depends what we focus on. As Dan Sullivan, founder of Strategic Coach, often says, 'the eyes and ears find what the brain is looking for'.

The whole legal system is based on this premise (that you can argue anything any which way, as long as you have evidence, and there's always evidence for most arguments, you just need to look for it). It's in this way (our RAS filtering in and out certain data) that our limiting beliefs become strengthened over time, because we continue to perceive evidence to reinforce and prove them. This means we accept them and often don't think to question or challenge them.

For example, if you believe that your writing skills are poor, then you're far more likely to zone in on the one spelling mistake you've made in a document rather than think about the other perfectly worded pages. If you don't think you're good at presenting, that one chart that you fumbled over will be the only thing you remember, not the other 38 perfectly delivered slides.

So, how can we move past our limiting beliefs when our brains are wired to reinforce them? The next chapter will show you how; this is where reframing techniques come in.

The gift of awareness is to see your programming, and then to be less dependent on heuristics. I think awareness is as natural to human beings as forming habits, but we just tend to focus on it less. We benefit less. Another topic is that of psychological safety and fear. Leaders can unlock potential in themselves if they lean into that and do the necessary inquiry.

– Tim Munden, Chief Learning Officer, Unilever

11 How to Reframe Limiting Beliefs

This is an exercise that you might find useful for contradicting a limiting belief that you hold, and replacing it with a more empowering and realistic one instead.

There are many different ways of challenging your limiting beliefs. For some people, just tuning into them and calling them out is enough to get back on track with more helpful thinking. However, for most of us, it will take a bit more practice. To train our thinking, it's always helpful to have a simple tool, until it becomes a more natural way for us to think.

Here is a five-minute tool you can use to help 'reframe' your thinking (Figure 11.1). If you want to download all the tools from this book in PDF format, visit www.symbiapartners.com/mentalfitnessresources. What I mean when I say 'reframe' is to give it a different perspective. You can use this tool for 'shared beliefs' or 'shared assumptions' that your team might have about a project, such as the prospects of success for your business or brand.

As I mentioned before, the tricky thing about beliefs is that they seem completely plausible to us, so we often don't think to challenge them and we accept them as a given. That's where we go wrong. This tool will help you see that the belief is just one version of the truth and that other, more helpful, versions exist.

Reframing Technique

It's really simple. You take the belief you currently have and put it at the top left of the template – for example, 'I'm not good enough to get promoted'. In the right-hand corner, write a more positive and possible expression of the belief. I don't want you to write the exact opposite (e.g. 'I *will* get promoted') because your brain will just reject it as you know you don't believe it. For example, a more positive and possible version might be, 'I have as much chance as anyone else to get promoted'. We just want to open up your brain to the possibility of another outcome.

Underneath, I want you to write down all the evidence for why the statement is true. Start with the one in the top left. This will be easy as you have been 'collecting' evidence to support it already. You might write:

- I don't think people rate my work.
- I'm not sure I have the right experience.
- I don't work on any of the interesting or high-profile projects.
- They're only promoting small numbers of people.
- I'm not good at self-promotion, I don't like it.
- The best way to get promoted is to work on the high-profile stuff and do an exceptional job.

Then I want you to go to the right-hand side and write all the evidence supporting that belief. This will be harder for you to do because, until now, you've been largely deleting a lot of this evidence and only seeing the evidence to support your other belief.

Because this part can be difficult, I recommend you give it a go and then ask a friend or colleague to help expand your thinking. You'll be surprised by some of the responses, and it will help you open your mind and also your perspective.

Evidence you might then have below this empowering version of the belief could be:

- The projects I work on might not be high profile, but I do get compliments and encouragement from my manager about the work I do.

- My experience is different from other people's, which can be an asset for the team if I leverage it.

- Three people have been promoted this year, so maybe there's more opportunity than I think.

- I've only been here a year, and I seem to be doing well.

- There are training programmes to help me fill in any gaps.

- People have been promoted who don't work on high-level projects but have shown a lot of effort and commitment to the job.

Once you have exhausted this list (and always try to make this second list of evidence longer than the first), go to the next row and answer the questions.

Now that you have looked at both sides, what's possible? You might write: 'If I put the effort into developing myself and show commitment and dedication, there is the opportunity to be promoted'.

Then answer the question: 'What are the action steps you should take to make this possibility a reality?' This is where you can identify the actions and steps you can take to make the goal of being promoted a reality. For example:

- I should speak to my manager and find out what they think I should focus on to get to the next level.

- I should explore the training courses available to me and sign up for at least one of them.

- I should ask if I can have a mentor to help my development and prepare me for promotion.

What is the limiting belief?	What is the 'opposite' belief?
I'm not good enough to get promoted	*Do not simply write the opposite, think about what the most positive and possible expression could be.* *I have as much chance as anyone else to get promoted*

List all the evidence to support it	List all the evidence to support it
• *I don't think people rate my work* • *I'm not sure I have the right experience* • *I don't work on any of the interesting or high-profile projects* • *They're only promoting small numbers of people* • *I'm not good at self-promotion, I don't like it* • *The best way to get promoted is to work on the high-profile stuff and really do an exceptional job*	*Here, we recommend you give it a go and then ask a family member, friend, or colleague to help expand your thinking.* • *The projects I work on might not be high-profile, but I do get compliments and encouragement from my manager about the work I do* • *My experience is different from other people which can be an asset for the team if I leverage it* • *3 people this year have been promoted, so maybe there's more opportunity than I think* • *I've only been here a year and I seem to be doing well* • *There are training programs to help me fill in any gaps* • *People have been promoted who don't work on high-level projects but have shown a lot of effort and commitment to the job*

What are the action steps you should take to make this possibility a reality?
• *I should speak to my manager and find out what they think I should focus on to get to the next level* • *I should explore the training courses available to me and sign up for at least one of them* • *I should ask if I can have a mentor to help develop me and prepare me for promotion*

Figure 11.1   Reframing your thinking.

Finally, fill in the answers to move you towards positive action:

- What can you do today?
- What can you do this week?
- What can you do for the next month?

(Tip: add a date for each of your actions and put them in order of when you will do them.)

What you are doing when you run through this exercise is overriding the RAS and opening up your ability to see the information you've been ignoring. This is just one way of challenging your beliefs and helping remove the sometimes invisible obstacles holding you back from making progress in life. There are many more tools which you can access at www.symbiapartners.com/mentalfitnessresources.

By developing new, positive habits, it's possible to 'rewire' your brain to move towards a growth mindset – and keep it there. Just practising one quick exercise each day for as little as three weeks is enough to make a lasting impact!

As I mentioned, this is also a great tool for teams to flush out any hidden beliefs that might be holding them back from success. You can do this in a group context by just recreating the template on a whiteboard or flipchart. Have someone in charge of the writing, and get everyone else to shout out the answers. Get people to generate as many things as possible until you can't come up with any more evidence.

If you don't yet know what limiting belief might be holding you back, then go back a step. Get a blank board or flipchart, and ask people to generate as many 'thoughts' or 'beliefs' as possible that could be holding the team back. Ask people to get as creative as possible; *nothing* is off limits. Usually the 'hidden' belief or evidence comes out towards the end of the brainstorming. It's rarely the first thing to jump out, and that's why it's important to keep going.

When I do this with groups, I always know when the limiting belief comes out because there's either a collective noise (a sigh, a laugh, or an ohhhh!) or it's just met with a complete, but knowing, silence. Once you've got *the* belief (or one or two of them), run it through the exercise above and see how it shifts your collective thinking. It's a very empowering and cathartic exercise for teams to complete.

> Resilience or mental fitness directly translates into effectiveness at work. You know, your ability to be gritty in life. If you learn how to work on mindset through professional sports, it can equally translate into the workplace – why would it not?
>
> *– Head of Wellbeing, Global Financial Services*

> [When you neglect mental fitness] you are putting your business at peril and you may not even know it. All the best stuff you've ever accomplished; all the biggest wins and breakthroughs; all the most pride-worthy results you have created – were all preceded by thoughts and feelings. Codifying those preceding thoughts and feelings is your job in the forensics of creating tomorrow's excellence.
>
> *– Matthew McCarthy, CEO, Ben & Jerry's*

Part Five
Values: Principles We Live By

Values are a concept that everybody seems to vaguely understand. Some instinctively know what their own personal values are. However, the reality is that most people don't properly understand the concept of values and have never truly done the work to understand what values they have (often unconsciously) chosen to live their lives by. I'm going to help you get clear on your values in the following chapters.

Your values are the principles that you're living your life by. You may have inherited them from family, friends, religion, or politics. Where they come from isn't what's important, but awareness of what they are is.

As with your beliefs, you need to know what your values are because they are influencing your decisions, whether you are aware of them or not. Once you become aware of your values, you can save yourself a lot of pain and time in the future because you can consciously use them as a filter for the big decisions in your life. Your values can accelerate you forward in those decisions. You can use them to help you navigate conflict. You can also use them to pre-empt situations that you might otherwise have to revisit due to a misinformed decision resulting from being completely unaware of your values.

In this part, I'll help you understand what your personal values are and the power they have. I'll share a number of real-life stories to show how an awareness of values has helped other people. I'll also share the impact they can have on teams and why co-creating your team values (and behaviours) can have a transformational impact.

12 Values and Decision Making

You know by now that the key to mental fitness is first learning about yourself, then learning how to optimise your inner game for performance. That's why we've taken you on a journey of self-awareness, helping you see how you see the world (perception), recognising the meaning we overlay onto events, and how that affects our thinking, emotions, and behaviours. Then we've drilled deeper into uncovering our beliefs and now our values. It's this foundational work that will allow us to fine-tune ourselves in the future. The 'fine-tuning' is self-regulation, our ability to mentally and emotionally step out of a situation before reacting; it's our intuition, that 'knowing' that there's a limiting belief working against us or showing up as resistance within our teams. It's here, in this 'knowing', that I believe wisdom lies.

When working with corporate teams, especially leadership teams, I always get people to work on uncovering their personal values. Although they like the idea of finding out a bit more about themselves, they don't always understand *why it matters*. I often get looks that say 'aren't we here to work on the team? Why am I looking at myself?' In many cases, people are also confused as to what exactly personal values are.

Let's face it, it's not as though we had a class on values in school. From time to time (but rarely) they might come up in conversation, but generally it's not a topic that is well discussed or understood. That's why it's worth first exploring why they matter so much, as well as how we can access them to accelerate decision-making, to navigate conflict, and to understand our 'gut feelings'.

So, what are values? Essentially they are concepts (ways of being and thinking) that we deem to be important. They tend to be represented by single words that are often high level, conceptual, and open to interpretation (which is why it's so important that we go a level deeper and explain what the value means to us) – examples include transparency, justice, bravery, and integrity.

Much like beliefs, we adopt values from our environment, what we are exposed to, what we learn from our family, religion, culture, and politics and our experiences in life.

Values are usually fairly stable, yet they don't have strict limits or boundaries. As we move through life, our values may (but not often) change. A good example of how they might shift can be found in your definition of success. It's very likely that your definition of success in your twenties versus your thirties versus your forties will have changed.

In your twenties, there's a tendency to be focused on money, usually because you've been scraping by since you were a student. In your thirties, it might be more about status and promotion as you attempt to climb the ladder. In your forties, success tends to become about meaning, purpose, and contribution.

As our definition of success changes, so do our personal values. This is why keeping in touch with our values is a lifelong exercise. We should continuously revisit them, especially if we start to feel unbalanced … and we can't quite figure out why.

Values underpin the basis for much of our behaviour. They are abstract and tend not to be obvious to people (even ourselves). They represent a combination of who we already are and who we want to be, so they can be aspirational (a way of life that we are striving for but not always able to get right). Because they can be abstract, it's really important to know what they mean to you.

Whether you uphold values of loyalty or truthfulness, charity, or service, you need to know how *you* actually define that word. Take creativity, for example. How I define creativity might be very different from how someone else would define it. For one person it might be very much about the arts and the ability to express their emotions through painting. However, for me it might be the ability to come up with lots of ideas and to be spontaneous when brainstorming an alternative during problem solving.

You see this problem occurring in relationships all the time, because you may think you have the same values as your colleague, your boss, or even your partner, and you may both have the same words for your values. However, what those words mean to each of you can sometimes be quite different. If you're ever sharing or discussing your values with someone else, make sure you qualify exactly what each value means for you and ask the other person to do the same. The key is to avoid assumptions.

When I ask people what they think their values are, whether in a workshop or an online programme, I usually hear the 'sexy' ones. These are the aspirational ones (e.g. freedom, creativity, autonomy, flexibility, and so on). Hardly anyone ever says security, consistency, or fairness (they aren't very aspirational). But they absolutely are people's values, and often they're deep-rooted, operational values that influence our decision making (Figure 12.1).

The difference is they just aren't front of mind. That's why *how* we uncover our values is as important as the exercise itself. To go deeper, you really need to be forced to 'trade off' your values (be forced to choose between pairs) to fully understand which ones, when it comes to the crunch, you really care about. I'll explain more about that during the exercise later.

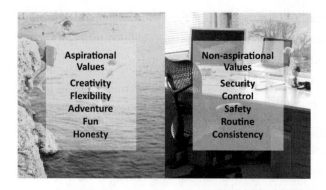

Figure 12.1   Aspirational versus non-aspirational values.

We shouldn't judge our values, though. They all bring meaning and help us live our lives in a certain way, and that matters (whether they are 'sexy' or not is irrelevant).

Let me share a story about Theresa. Theresa had a very successful marketing career; she was a vice president of a billion-dollar brand in one of the biggest marketing companies in the world. We met during a leadership session I was running (she was one of the participants), and she contacted me afterwards to see if I did private coaching. I tend not to do much these days as I much prefer working with groups, but I'll always make an exception for an interesting challenge.

Theresa was in her early 40s with a big life goal: to run her own successful business, after running so many successful brands for big corporations. She had indeed attempted to do so twice with no success and had returned to employment. The first attempt didn't go well because of the 2008 economic crisis; the second one was blamed on a weak business plan.

Now she had come to me for coaching and consultancy around her new business plan in preparation for the third attempt. After years of working with big corporates and a background in market research and marketing, I was very tempted to do just that and focus on her business plan.

Instead of talking about the business plan, though, we did a values elicitation exercise. This is because when there is a 'pattern' showing up in your life, it's a clue to a continued unmet value need. After 30 minutes, we were able to identify that one of Theresa's core operational values was 'security'.

Now, security and entrepreneurship don't exactly go hand in hand. That doesn't mean you can't be an entrepreneur if security is a value of yours, but it does mean that you need that value to be met elsewhere. This is the issue with values: if they are not getting met, you will be miserable, and you'll eventually quit that job, relationship, team – because you feel compromised or that 'something just isn't right'.

As I've mentioned though, the word 'security' can be ambiguous. It means different things to different people, which is why you always need to drill down one layer deeper. For one person it might mean a job with the same company for 40 years, for another it might mean a long-term loving relationship, and for someone else it might be related to money. For Theresa it represented money.

The next line of questioning was: What do you need financially to feel secure? Is it about pensions, investments, equity, cash in the bank? For Theresa it was cash in the bank.

How much cash in the bank do you need to have in order to feel secure? This is the amount Theresa needed so that when she hit the inevitable bumps in the road that come from starting a business, she wouldn't go running back into employment. The answer: £50 000. Brilliant. That's the goal.

The goal is not to have a watertight business plan; as nice as it sounds, they don't exist, and curveballs will always laugh at your business plan. What matters is that you have a sound business plan *and* the wherewithal to mentally and emotionally withstand the ups and downs of entrepreneurship. So, that became Theresa's goal.

For the next two years her focus was on saving enough money to feel that she had a 'cushion'. In that time I also encouraged her to experiment (while remaining in her corporate job) with the business plan on a hobby basis to get a feel for whether it would work and if she actually enjoyed the 'side hustle'. Both strategies meant that by the time she eventually went 100% in, she was much more confident in her ability to make it a success *and* her value of security was already being met. I'm happy to say five years on, Theresa is still in business and hasn't looked back.

When making decisions about your future, knowing your values can save you years of trial and error. Where I tend to see them impact the most is in career choice, business decisions, relationships, and, of course, teams (which are just networked relationships). If you're unhappy working in a team, working on a particular project, brand, or business, and you can't quite put your finger on why, it's worthwhile looking at your values and checking whether they're being met or if they're being challenged. For the last five years we've taken probably 5000 execs on the journey of helping them identify their personal purpose. The majority of those people (but not all) were Unilever employees – because purpose is at the core of everything they do. Anyone in the branding and marketing world knows Unilever ensures all of their brands have a societal impact – they have a bigger purpose beyond selling more product. But what you might not know is that having people with purpose is just as important to them. Because the data tells us that not only are people with purpose more resilient, they can more easily navigate change and are more engaged in the work they do. Besides this, they are just more fulfilled as employees and their retention is high. How does this relate to values? Well, in order to uncover your personal purpose you can't *not* know your personal values. They are integral to your larger purpose.

How Do Our Values and Beliefs Differ?

Beliefs and values are different concepts. Values represent our aims and our desires for how we want to live our lives. Beliefs, on the other hand, are rules we have made up based on our capabilities, views of the world, or attitudes towards ourselves or other people. Both values and beliefs shape our map of the world and our perception of what is going on around us. They act as filters on our perception and, as such, it's really important to understand them as they are also the key to shifting our perceptions of the world and thus our experience of it.

Beliefs versus Values

Beliefs	Values
Set of rules	Single abstract words
Come from real experiences that we have interpreted	Principles, standards, or qualities that an individual holds in high regard
Affect the quality of our work and all of our relationships because what you believe is what you experience	Guide the way we live our lives and the decisions we make
We tend to think that our beliefs are based on reality, but it is our beliefs that govern our experiences	A value can be defined as something that we hold dear or qualities that we consider to be of worth

Benefits of Knowing Your Values When Making Business Decisions

Knowing your core values allows you to make effective decisions in life and in business. They are already an unconscious filter by which you make decisions, but they can become a much more helpful *conscious* filter to help you make decisions about your career, relationships, health, finance, and all other aspects of life. They help you understand why you do the things you do.

If you know your values upfront, you can use them to help you when you are making important decisions, such as about whom to recruit into your team, whether to go for that promotion, or whether to move countries. To use your values for decision making, you should assess the options by comparing how many of your values each one meets. Look at which values each option doesn't meet and work out if that's a deal-breaker.

We can also use our values to improve our relationships and navigate conflict. You see, when we are in a disagreement with someone, without information, our tendency is to assume that our disagreement is personal or at the very least due to differing personalities. What's so helpful about knowing our values (and the values of the people we work with) is that this knowledge helps us have a different conversation.

I was once running a three-day workshop with a leadership team in a globally renowned telecommunications company, and during the break a side conversation occurred about the next promotion opportunity for moving someone from a senior manager role to director level. The conversation was quite heated because the two men speaking were in disagreement about who should be promoted. The conversation went something like this:

'The obvious choice is Henry, he's been here for 15 years, he's dedicated and knows the company processes so well'.

'I can see that Henry is strong, but the truth is Geetha is so much better suited to this role than Henry. I know she's not been here long, but she's sharp, she's hungry, and I think she will really challenge us'.

'I don't understand why you're being so dismissive of Henry. We hardly know Geetha, what signal do we send to people if she's just in the door and gets promoted?'

'We will be communicating that we value talent, that if you work hard, you get promoted! Geetha is crushing it, she's come in here, questioned and shaken up our processes, she's doing things none of us have thought of and it's making a real difference'.

And so the conversation continued. Each one defending their candidate and taking it personally when they couldn't persuade the other to see it their way (remember perception?!).

The great thing was that we were about to go into our 'Values Poker' session, and I made sure they were both in the same small group. At the end of the session (which usually takes about an hour), the leaders shared their values with everyone – I wanted to use it as an example of how we can use our values to understand behaviours, preferences, and positions in arguments.

In the top four values of one of the leaders was 'loyalty'; the other leader had 'pioneering' in theirs. No prize for guessing that the leader who valued loyalty was championing Henry, who'd been there 15 years, and the leader championing Geetha (who was leading the way with new initiatives) valued pioneering.

So who's right? They both are.

The point isn't about who is right and who is wrong. The point is that understanding values helps us move beyond surface-level discussions to understand what we are really debating. The conversation is then not about what's more important – your value of loyalty or my value of pioneering – but instead you get to ask, what are the right values needed for this role?

The next step would then be to understand the values of the candidates and to make your selection based on what the role needs and who the candidate is – not just allow the 'lens' of the leaders (their personal values influencing their candidate choice) to be the only factor that matters.

It's worth noting that our careers don't need to fulfil all of our values, but our lives do. Let's take an example: fun. Most careers tend not to be high on the 'fun factor', but if you have a great social life and every weekend you are doing fun things with your family or friends, that value is getting met, so it's less important in your career. We just need to know that our values are getting met somewhere because if they're not, it will lead to a feeling that something is missing.

We can *feel* our values, both when they're in alignment and when they're not. In our workshops with teams, I always get people to look back at a period in their career or life when they were unhappy. With the new knowledge and clarity of their values, I get them to post-analyse which value or values were missing. It's always a massive light bulb moment for people.

We typically default to logical and rational reasons for being unsatisfied/unhappy: the salary wasn't high enough, the boss was difficult, excessive stress, etc. We don't always realise that *variety* is a core driving value of ours, and we accidentally ended up in quite a predictable and routine job, which led us to feelings of boredom and being under-utilised and undervalued, which caused us to leave.

I constantly tell clients that we *feel* our values, whether we are aware of their existence or not. We feel them when they're being met (satisfied, fulfilled, aligned), and we feel them even more strongly when they're not. When values aren't met, it's called incongruence. This usually makes us feel uncomfortable, unhappy, or heavy, as though something's missing or wrong.

Have you ever had a sinking feeling in your stomach, but you're not sure why? Has a decision been made at work which makes you feel uneasy, angry or disappointed? Have you heard a story about something that upsets you beyond belief?

This may indicate that there's an incongruence with one of your values. It feels uncomfortable and just wrong. When you get this unsettling feeling, look at your values, look at the situation, and understand which value is being challenged. You'll use language like:

'Something just isn't sitting right with me'.

'I'm uncomfortable with this'.

'I can feel in my gut that it's wrong'.

This is where negative patterns come from in our relationships or our career choices. It's because we are making decisions that are incongruent or the opposite of what our value needs are.

For example, you've got very upset with a colleague over the fact that they've not given you credit for work you've done. People can see that you should be a little upset, but you are uncharacteristically annoyed about it. You wish it didn't annoy you so much, and you wonder why you are so upset. But when you know that *justice* is a core driving value for you, you can recognise you're upset because someone has violated this value.

Now you can have a different conversation. You can explain your values, what's important to you in life and why what happened is so upsetting. Values help to make sense of conflict, both for yourself and for the people you are in conflict with. Values can be a massive key to unlocking issues when you know how to identify them and when there is an incongruence (they are being violated) or when there is integrity (your values are being met). See Figure 12.2.

If patterns are showing up in your life, it's a clue. For example, maybe you notice that after a year you always get a bit jaded in your role? Or working in a team, if you're not the leader, you become disengaged? Or maybe you feel like your line reports always take up too much of your time? Perhaps you tend to meet the same challenges in your relationships, even if it's with different people? Maybe you

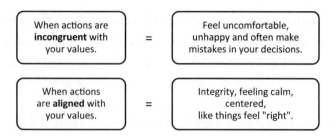

Figure 12.2   Recognising incongruence.

always end up arguing over the same things? Or the same problems always come up? This means you need to look at your values, as it's likely there is an incongruence somewhere within them.

Importance of Establishing Team Values

As you can see, knowing your values significantly improves decision making, and it's worth knowing that decision-making efficiency is pretty much always an area that the leadership teams we work with get feedback on during the diagnosis phase. Basically, teams want to see their leaders (and everyone really) making decisions swiftly, ones that keep them on course and don't get 'reopened' a week later. Besides the fact that it helps with decision-making efficiency, there are many other benefits to teams becoming clear about their values:

- Values support teams in the decision-making process.
- Values also help teams prioritise how to respond to opportunities and challenges.
- Agreeing on a set of shared values and behaviours means consciously discussing what you expect from each other as a team.
- When you agree to a set of team values, you are also committing to demonstrating them, so they act as a form of 'shared contract'.
- Being clear about a team's values and behaviours makes it easier to point out poor or unacceptable behaviour without becoming overly personal.

- Above all, the process of agreeing on values means that teams have important conversations about expectations and behaviour that they might not normally have.

You'll notice the word 'behaviours' appearing in the list above. That's because values can sometimes feel too conceptual and are open to interpretation. It's fine to stay at just the value word when only one person needs to know what it means (e.g. personal values), but when they are shared, it's best not to leave things open to interpretation. Therefore, it's important to be clear about the behaviours that bring those values to life. This allows you to define exactly what you expect (and don't expect) from people.

Usually in our sessions we always leave the Vision, Purpose, and Values work until the last day. This is when we focus on the future, on everything that's now possible (since the last two days are usually spent acknowledging and removing obstacles to performance). Before we get into the creative phase of generating team values and behaviours, I always let people know that we will be working in small groups and that it will take at least three iterations. That's because the most important part is what happens in the conversations. Yes, having an inspiring and aligned set of values and behaviours is the objective, but the conversations people have to have with each other to get there is the real game changer. This is when people empty out all of the assumptions in their head onto the table. You get to hold things up, point at them, and ask: is this who we want to be? Do we need to change this? This is the moment when teams start to enhance their collective mental fitness, because they're raising awareness of the assumptions in their minds. There's always a shift in energy at the end of these sessions because there's a feeling that everything has just 'clicked' together. They've been able to address topics which before felt somewhat taboo or personal (people's ideals and behaviours) without having to offend anyone and consequently inspire each other instead.

I worked with a leadership team in the haircare category a few years ago in North America. They were facing some real challenges of trust which was affecting communication, team morale, collaboration, and more. We spent three days working together on the barriers holding them back. On the afternoon of the last day, we worked on team values and behaviours. The session was profound, for a number of reasons. When they shared at the end, one of the leaders couldn't hold back their emotion, saying they just felt an overwhelming sense of relief to finally have (what they felt) the solution to so many of the challenges they'd experienced over the last 10 years. The solution was ultimately an 'agreement' on how they were and weren't going to behave with each other. Of course, this isn't the solution: what you need is for people to follow through on their commitments. But as she had expressed it on that day: 'this just gives me hope, that what we want to achieve is finally possible'. As I said before, the values and behaviours themselves aren't the answer, but they catalyse important conversations which often aren't happening with teams – it's that transparency that can make a difference. Below are the values and behaviours the leadership team came up with.

Trust

Communicate regularly and often.

Be authentic and transparent.

Make it safe for every single person to be heard.

Admit your mistakes and learn together.

Hold ourselves and each other accountable.

Ask for help.

Deal fairly and with integrity.

Entrepreneurial

Take risks. Break rules.

Challenge everything, but know when to move on.

Be hungry and get after it.

Engage in purposeless curiosity and seek outside inspiration.

Stay agile through growth.

Approach everything with a beginner's spirit.

One Team

Win together. No one left behind.

All hands on deck. Always.

Accept and embrace our differences.

Recognize the team.

Celebrate the wins.

Support and push each other.

Passion

Love what you do, *so much*.

Creativity is our lifeblood.

Own it. Do it.

Execute with pride.

Always be professional.

There's an issue in many organisations that they focus too much on competencies. Competencies are important, but the idea of mastering the self (or personal mastery) not only benefits the individual, but also the organisation because you've got a group of people who are striving for mastery but who are also becoming real experts in what they're doing.

– *Dr David Wilkinson, Editor-in-Chief of the* Oxford Review

13 Uncovering Your Values

As I said earlier, if I were to ask you, 'What are your values?' you would likely come up with a list of your idealistic (aspirational) values. They are the values you want to have and the ones you think are important. However, they might not be the ones you're 'operating' from (in other words, the ones influencing your decisions), and that's why going through a values exercise thoroughly is very important.

There are many different types of values exercises. The one I have here separates the values that you aspire to have from the ones that are already influencing your decisions. We call these your operational values.

When I work with teams, I use our 'Values Poker' card game as a fun but effective way of helping people identify their values and share reflections and anecdotes from their lives to help other people understand the context and driving forces behind their values. It's one of our most popular exercises because it allows for a certain amount of vulnerability without making people feel overly exposed. We run it face to face and also virtually (yes, we can recreate a poker table online, and it works surprisingly well). The game allows people to get to know each other at a more human level, to hear anecdotes from their lives, and understand the context in which a person is showing up to work. These conversations create a deeper connection between people and ultimately build empathy and understanding, which, of course, are the foundations that trust is built on. Never underestimate the importance of sharing your story with the people you work with. That's how we enhance the collective mental fitness of the team, by people connecting first with their own inner game and then to the inner game of their teammates – this is the hidden edge to team performance.

In workshops, as we build up to the Values Poker game, from time to time I'll have people pull me aside at the coffee break asking not to be in the same group as someone or mentioning that two people have a difficult relationship and so advise me to put them at different tables. All that means is that they should definitely be in a group together, because they *need* this deeper understanding of each other. The benefit absolutely outweighs the risk; I've never regretted it. Too often we default to blaming personality as a reason for why people don't get on, when more often than not it's because they have different worldviews and often different values. When you get the chance to see that and understand someone's behaviours through the lens of their values, it changes your perception. Suddenly you don't take it personally any more, because there is a deeper understanding of why the person is the way they are.

Let me bring that to life for you through an example. I was working with the CEO of an aviation company and their senior exec team. The CFO was typically seen as very controlling with money, never wanting people to spend their budgets and counting every penny in the business – which, to be fair, is an excellent attribute for a CFO. It's great for business but not always good for relationships. When playing Values Poker, the CFO described his childhood and how impoverished it was.

He revealed that growing up, his family often went to bed hungry, rarely had meat, milk, or cheese and largely got by on potatoes and grains. Most of his life he lived in poverty, but his father prioritised his education and, by candlelight every night, he dedicated hours to teaching him to read. He went on to get a scholarship, go to college, become an accountant, and eventually become a CFO.

But, he had vowed to himself and his family that he would never let them go into poverty again and that he would do the best he could do for any employer he worked with to ensure their money was safe.

There was a silence. Slowly the other people in his group shared how grateful they were that he had told this story because, until that moment, they just thought he was 'difficult', 'tight', and all of the other bad associations. It wasn't until this story, and the realisation that security was a core driver of his, that they realised why he behaved the way he did and why counting every penny was so important to him. His behaviour suddenly made sense to people and was seen as a good quality. That's how powerful our personal story can be in helping people understand why we are the way we are. Too often I see teams fall into dysfunction because they operate at the level of assumption; they let too much go unsaid and don't have the right conversations. At the same time, they are charged with running successful businesses, building brands, and disrupting categories. This is usually happening in suboptimal conditions. Just imagine what is possible when your teams not only work on their own mental fitness but begin to work on their collective mental fitness; when they become aware of the narratives and beliefs they've created about each other, about the marketplace, about your competitors; when they understand that the inner game is as important as the outer game, that's when the game starts to get played at a different level.

Uncovering Your Values

This exercise aims to take you through six steps to uncover your personal values. These values will be based on your personal experiences of happiness, pride, and fulfilment, ensuring you are truly uncovering what's at your core. If you're interested on working on your team's values and behaviours, contact us at www.symbipartners.com, and we'll share a toolkit for you and your team.

The steps below outline how we will work to explore and refine your values:

1. Identify the times when you were **happiest**.
2. Identify the times when you were most **proud**.
3. Identify the times when you were most **fulfilled and satisfied**.
4. **Determine** your top values, based on your experiences of happiness, pride, and fulfilment.
5. **Prioritise** your top values.
6. **Reaffirm** your values.

1. Identify the times when you were happiest

Use examples from both your career and personal life to ensure there is balance in your answers.

- What were you doing?
- Were you with other people? Who?
- What other factors contributed to your happiness?
- What did the experience give you a sense of?
- What was it about the experience that made you feel happy?

2. Identify the times when you were most proud

- Why were you proud?
- Did other people share your pride? Who?

- What other factors contributed to your feelings of pride?
- What were the characteristics you displayed to get you to that point?

3. Identify the times when you were most fulfilled and satisfied

- What need or desire was fulfilled?
- How and why did the experience give your life meaning?
- What other factors contributed to your feelings?

4. Determine your top values, based on your experiences of happiness, pride, and fulfilment

Think about why each experience was truly important and memorable.

Then, using the list on the following page to help you, choose the values that resonate with you. Be sure to include ones that are being communicated in your answers in Steps 1–3. You are not limited to the list; feel free to add your own. Language matters when it comes to values, so pick the words which resonate most with you.

As you work through, you may find that some of these values naturally combine. For instance, if you value philanthropy, community, and generosity, you might say that service to others is one of your top values.

(continued)

(continued)

Example values

Accountability	Determination	Hard work
Accuracy	Devoutness	Health
Achievement	Diligence	Helping
Adventure	Discipline	Holiness
Altruism	Discretion	Honesty
Ambition	Diversity	Honour
Art	Dynamism	Independence
Assertiveness	Economy	Integrity
Awareness	Effectiveness	Knowledge
Balance	Efficiency	Laughter
Being the best	Elegance	Learning
Belonging	Empathy	Love
Boldness	Enjoyment	Loyalty
Calmness	Enthusiasm	Money
Carefulness	Equality	Nature
Challenge	Excellence	Openness
Cheerfulness	Excitement	Order
Clear-mindedness	Expertise	Patience
Commitment	Exploration	Power
Community	Expressiveness	Recognition
Compassion	Fairness	Relationships
Competitiveness	Faith	Religion
Connection	Fame	Responsibility
Consistency	Family-centredness	Reward
Contentment	Fidelity	Risk-taking
Continuous	Fitness	Security
improvement	Fluency	Self-respect
Contribution	Focus	Serenity
Control	Friendship	Spirituality
Cooperation	Freedom	Spontaneity
Correctness	Fun	Stability
Courtesy	Generosity	Status
Creativity	Goodness	Success
Curiosity	Grace	Time
Decisiveness	Growth	Truth
Democracy	Happiness	Understanding
Dependability		

5. Prioritise your top values

Of the values you chose in Step 4, you will now choose 12 of them to represent your top values (or operational values). You will then organise them in order of importance to you.

This will likely be difficult, because you'll have to look deep inside yourself. However, this is important because, when making a decision, you'll have to choose between solutions that may satisfy different values. This is when you must know which value is more important to you.

1. _____   7. _____

2. _____   8. _____

3. _____   9. _____

4. _____   10. _____

5. _____   11. _____

6. _____   12. _____

Select the top six from this list that you can't do without. It will be difficult to choose six at first, so create sets of two (e.g. autonomy versus security) and ask yourself which one is the more important of the two. A way to do this is to imagine that you have a job offer that has autonomy but NO security, and equally another job offer that has security but NO autonomy – you have to pick one, which one do you choose?

(continued)

(continued)

Keep doing this with all the values until you end up with the final six. It will be difficult but well worth it.

Next, look again at each value you have listed in the previous table. Answer the question: 'Which is more important to me – number 1 or 2?' If you answer number 1, circle the number 1 in the first column. Then repeat the process for every one of the values: 1-3, 1-4, 1-5, and so on, until 11-12. Work quickly. *Some values may overlap, but that's fine; make a choice anyway.* It might also help to visualise a situation where you might have to make that choice.

Trading off your values:

1-2 2-3 3-4 4-5 5-6 6-7 7-8 8-9 9-10 10-11 11-12
1-3 2-4 3-5 4-6 5-7 6-8 7-9 8-10 9-11 10-12
1-4 2-5 3-6 4-7 5-8 6-9 7-10 8-11 9-12
1-5 2-6 3-7 4-8 5-9 6-10 7-11 8-12
1-6 2-7 3-8 4-9 5-10 6-11 7-12
1-7 2-8 3-9 4-10 5-11 6-12
1-8 2-9 3-10 4-11 5-12
1-9 2-10 3-11 4-12
1-10 2-11 3-12
1-11 2-12
1-12

Now count up the number of circles for each value. This is your weighted score. Write down the scores next to each value in the list from Step 5. They are now ranked in order of *actual* importance, not 'aspirational' importance.

6. Reaffirm your values

Check your top-priority values, and make sure they fit with your life and your vision for yourself by answering the questions below:

- Do these values make you feel good about yourself?
- Are you proud of your top three values?
- Would you be comfortable and proud to tell your values to people you respect and admire?
- Do these values represent things you would support, even if your choice isn't popular and it puts you in a minority?
- After you've shortlisted your values (try not to have more than 4 or 5 or you'll never remember them), a good stress test is to share them with someone close to you. They'll tell you in a heartbeat if you've got the right ones or not. It always makes for a good conversation.

Identifying and understanding your values is a challenging but critical exercise. Your personal values are an essential part of who you are and also who you want to be. By becoming more aware of these important factors, life will be easier.

We're developing awareness of what, within the heart, really motivates you and how you bring that to the situation you're in. We're building awareness of personal mastery, of what your edge is, what your challenges are and what mental and emotional makeup you need to work with. Thinking about the future, we're building an awareness of our world, of how the world is shifting, of how you have mental models and skills, and how you need to adapt those to the world that you're in. I think awareness is the deep capability of the inner game.

— *Tim Munden, Chief Learning Officer, Unilever*

14 Using Values to Navigate Conflict

When you consider your values in decision making, you can be sure that the decisions you make will be in line with your sense of integrity and what you know is right. You will then be able to approach decisions with confidence and clarity. You'll also know that what you're doing is best for your current and future happiness and satisfaction.

Making values-based choices may not always be easy. However, making a choice that you know is right is a lot less difficult in the long run.

Using Values for Decision Making

We tend to make decisions through reason and logic, sometimes with subconscious (or conscious) belief systems and often using intuition. Few of us actually use values for decision making, usually because of the lack of awareness of our values in the first place.

But many of life's decisions are ultimately about determining what you value most. When many options seem reasonable, it's helpful and comforting to rely on your values – and use them as a strong guiding force to point you in the right direction. In business, using values is essential for efficient decision making.

Values-based decision making allows us to avoid being distracted by external factors that may sway our decision making (e.g. societal expectations, expectations of competitors, shareholders, etc.). They help us make informed decisions based on what's important to us in *advance*, so we don't have to learn *after* the fact that our values aren't getting met.

In addition, values-based analysis is a very useful tool to understand if values are at the core of conflict as opposed to something else. Our tendency as humans is to take things personally and attribute challenges among our team members, or between line reports and managers, to 'personality clashes'. In taking this approach, we often do ourselves a disservice. There can be many variables influencing things, from culture and differing world views, to perception differences and, of course, values.

My team and I were working with a marketing team in the a marketing team at Unilever, where they had extremely stretching targets and very little time within which to achieve them. The team were working hard but didn't seem to be getting anywhere. The vice president of the team called us in as she'd noticed some challenges with the team, in terms of projects being delivered late, inconsistent reasons being given for why advertising campaigns weren't ready when they should have been, and a general bad vibe from the team that she couldn't put her finger on.

The vice president asked us to help get the team to a place of health and high performance in order to meet their business targets, as they were quickly running out of time.

As with all our projects, we started with a diagnosis phase to understand what was really going on. My team and I ran one-on-one interviews (completely confidential to ensure they were open and honest) with everyone in the team, and it quickly became clear that there was a problem between the director of the brand and the most senior marketing manager. It was the tension between them that was affecting the energy and motivation of the whole team.

Before moving on to the next stage, which would have been a two-to three-day team session, I asked for six weeks to work one-on-one with the director and the senior manager (first separately and later together). The private coaching conversations usually began with frustration, finger pointing, character criticism, and so on. This is normal; people need to let off steam before being able to raise self-awareness.

The director was complaining that the senior manager only cared about timelines and didn't really put enough thought into whether the concepts, packaging design, or brand campaign (whatever it was they were working on) was good enough in the first place. It just looked as though she cared more about the delivery dates of work than the work itself.

On the flipside, the senior manager was frustrated because she felt the director was too detail orientated, was a bit of a perfectionist and, because of this, had no regard for deadlines or milestones and would prefer to keep 'tinkering' with things to get them perfect than be respectful of the deadlines. Both parties were frustrated with each other, and it often meant their communication was fractured, with each one feeling that the other 'didn't care'.

What struck me was that they actually both wanted to do a good job and they weren't deliberately trying to annoy each other. The problem was that they had differing definitions of what a 'good job' actually meant.

When we see conflict between people but a clear alignment on the outcome, there is usually an underlying values issue. Rather than spend more time focusing on the relationship, I worked with each of them separately to uncover their core drivers and see if there were any that might have been contributing to the underlying friction between them. I was not disappointed.

Within the director's top values was 'quality' in the number one spot. For the senior manager 'integrity' took the top spot in her core values. On the surface it didn't look like an obvious conflict; indeed, 'quality' and 'integrity' looked like complementary values. But as I've said before, we always need to drill down an extra layer to know how a specific value shows up for a person at the behavioural level.

What was most interesting was that 'integrity' for the senior manager meant 'keeping one's word'. That meant if she agreed to a deadline or a milestone, she was going to put all of her efforts into keeping her promise and delivering on that date. The problem occurred in the relationship because the director was less concerned with dates, deadlines, and milestones (and because of her seniority she also had more influence to move these anyway) – she was much more focused on whether the work being delivered was the best it could be, that they'd put the right resources, effort, and quality of thinking into the output. It was really clear they were both working with the best intentions for the business, but they were unknowingly 'rubbing' each other up the wrong way while they were doing it, which was affecting the whole team.

After the one-on-one sessions, I then brought them together for a paired session and shared what I had learned about each of their values – then I asked them to consider each of their values and how they might have influenced some of their discussions and even arguments.

It was a massive light-bulb moment for both of them, especially the realisation that they both just wanted to do a good job, but how they got there and what that meant looked different for each of them. Realising that the other person wasn't just being 'difficult' or trying to sabotage the project, but that they were actually extremely motivated to do a good job, went a long way towards easing tensions.

There was a palpable, if inaudible, sigh of relief in the room. This then made way for us to have a different conversation. Now that they both accepted that they wanted the same thing but their values were driving them towards different decisions, we were able to have a conversation about how to get the best out of these differing values and also how to navigate future potential conflict (which was really the same question).

They were both able to recognise that sometimes speed trumps quality and sometimes the reverse is true. So, they agreed that at the beginning of each project briefing they would align on what was more important, what would be the minimum number of quality checks they would put in place to ensure it didn't hinder speed, and *how*, *when*, and importantly *what* corners they would be allowed to cut.

Taking the conversation away from the personal (it's her/his fault) and being able to have a values conversation changed everything. The fact that we can point at values, explain what they mean, how they show up, and what it feels like when they are compromised allows for a less emotionally charged conversation and helps us navigate to solutions. After this work, we brought the team together for a three-day working session, and people were totally shocked at how well the director and senior manager were getting on with each other.

After three months, I went back and spoke to a handful of the team to see how the dynamics were – they said they were completely different! The director and senior manager were even able to poke fun at their values and constantly used them in discussions to make decisions. It had lifted the tension because there was no fault, just understanding, which changed the dynamic of the team for everyone. This is team mental fitness in action. Yes, business plans, budget, strategy, big campaign ideas, and so on are all important. But if your team don't have the right mindset and behaviours to work effectively together, the best strategy in the world won't help.

I know it's controversial to say that mental fitness is the only advantage that matters in business; it's deliberately controversial to encourage the debate. But after working with teams in business for 20 years, I know first-hand that if they don't have their 'inner game' sorted, any and all other advantages are wasted on them.

When leaders, teams, or companies do the work to identify their core values, they're forced to really examine and consider what they're doing and why it's so important. It also allows you to talk about the behaviours that really matter to the team and those that are unhelpful, distracting, or dysfunctional. What's more important is that it lets you address behavioural issues without having to point fingers or cast blame.

As I've said before, it's even more important though for a team to dig beyond the value (the one-word concept) and explain exactly what that means in terms of behaviours. Doing this means a team can align on, and commit to, how they are going to show up for each other. Later down the line, if issues arise, the values can be used as a way of calling out the behaviour that's not working and isn't aligned to the agreed values – meaning you can get back on track without unnecessary drama.

We have an interactive way of doing this with teams which is a lot of fun. As I always explain to the teams we work with, the end values and behaviours you create are excellent tools for helping each other navigate difficult situations, but what's more important than the output is the input.

The rounds of deep conversations they have to have in order to get to a final set of aligned values – it's these conversations that really make the difference. The level of truthfulness and transparency accessed means the team naturally accelerates their trust levels, which is, of course, a priceless benefit of the process.

Team values can then become their collective 'North Star' to centre around, a guide to measure themselves and aspects of their work by. They're a way to hold each other accountable without pointing fingers and also a new and fresh way to recruit new talent into the team. The benefits are really endless!

If you don't empower people to bring their best selves, their best inner game, mentally and emotionally, then the only lever you're pulling is the 'skill' lever. It's like giving people a luxury pen, but they haven't got the skills and muscles in their hand and the rest of their arm to do the writing. I think the number one issue is that you're missing the opportunity. You're leaving the value of your company on the table. The second thing is you're leaving energy and motivation, by not really encouraging people to bring all of themselves to work. Therefore, you're also allowing creativity, innovation, purposefulness, passion and connectivity to go to waste when these are actually critical for an organisation to succeed in the 21st century.

– Tim Munden, Chief Learning Officer, Unilever

Part Six
Stress and Performance

Every step of the way, so far, has been about enhancing your self-awareness and your ability to regulate and manage your thoughts, feelings, and actions. If you do everything I've already shared with you in this book well, it can only improve your performance and experience of life and business. However, none of us are superhuman; we're all still susceptible to experiencing moments of stress in life. Even if, through practice, most of the time we are managing ourselves, there will always be unexpected moments in life that can raise our stress levels, no matter how composed we are!

In this final section of the book, I'll look at both stress and performance and give you some long-term habits and immediate practical exercises that you can do when you're feeling as though you're in a hot state (or triggered, anxious, and stressed).

I'm also going to help you understand performance and how a little bit of stress is actually good for performance. I'll show you how and why the right level of stress can get you into a state of flow, but how too much stress will diminish your performance. Stress and performance are intrinsically linked, so it's important to understand both of these dimensions in order to get yourself into a place of sustained peak performance. I've also given you a toolkit just for this section. There are a variety of tools and practices you can implement and share with your teams.

15 Stress and Control

As part of the foundations of mental fitness, I always include some teaching around how we manage and relate to stress and pressure, and how that affects our performance. The combination of our perception, thinking, emotions, beliefs, and values will either result in us performing at our best or responding to life's challenges by being stressed and anxious. We all have good days and bad days, so it's important that if we find ourselves in a place of stress or anxiety (day-to-day anxiety, not clinical anxiety) that we know what to do about it.

We aren't always that attuned to what triggers stress for us as individuals and as teams. Yes, deadlines – sure, but what are the unexpected triggers that build up over time, and what can we do about them?

Let's start with a small reflection exercise. Take a few minutes and write down all the things that create stress and pressure in your life. Write until you can't think of any more; they can be both professional and personal, anything at all that raises your heart rate!

I ask this question all the time in my workshops and webinars, and the typical answers I get are

- Unexpected obstacles
- Deadlines
- Tight budgets

- Limited resources
- Demanding boss
- Changing objectives
- Personal obligations
- Being pulled in too many directions
- No time to think/plan

We all have stressors in our lives. The key is not to eliminate stress, but instead to find the ways in which to manage it, and its associated emotions, in a healthy and productive way.

Pressure and stress are unavoidable, and we deal with a variety of these on a daily basis in one way or another. However, the ability to understand the nature of stress and recognise our reaction to it when it's happening is what's needed to manage its impact on us both mentally and physically. *If you're expending energy on irrelevant things or negative thought patterns, you're taxing your brain unnecessarily and wasting this precious resource.*

Stress is not necessarily the result of the heavy workload, the demanding boss, or the 'traffic jam' of unfinished projects. It occurs *when the demands of a situation exceed our perceived ability to control them.* The more you perceive you can control, the lower your stress levels, and vice versa.

It's very important to know what you have influence and control over in your life to determine how and when to react to stress. When you control a situation, you influence the outcome. Every time you exercise control, you determine what happens in your brain, body, and the situation itself. In a confident and calm state, you work faster, solve problems more easily, and make fewer mistakes.

We can create immediate and dramatic shifts in our effectiveness and stress level by exerting control in small situations throughout the day. But before we can do that, we need to be able to determine what we can and can't control, along with what we can and can't influence.

Changing Our Relationship with Stress

Allowing stress to take over can inflict direct damage on our career, relationships, and well-being. But when taken as something to learn from, stress can be

- A great motivator
- A source of strength
- A survival instinct that pushes us beyond our perceived limits

Stress is experienced internally, and, as such, changing your response to it is actually within your ability – if you know how.

Now, you may have seen this concept before, perhaps as circles, but I like to use a matrix so you can then map your stressors out and they are visible to you (Figure 15.1).

The matrix is simple. At the bottom left, we have No Control and No Influence. At the top right, we have Control and Influence, and at the bottom right, we have Influence but No Control.

I'd like you to take the list of your stressors that you wrote down earlier, and take the time to map them out on the matrix. Are these things you have control over or not? If not, do you have influence? Remember the top left quadrant is void because you never have control and no influence. So, just focus on the other three quadrants.

Make sure to challenge your first thinking on this, because sometimes we believe that we have more control than we really do over things. At other times we think we have no control when actually we *do* have some control.

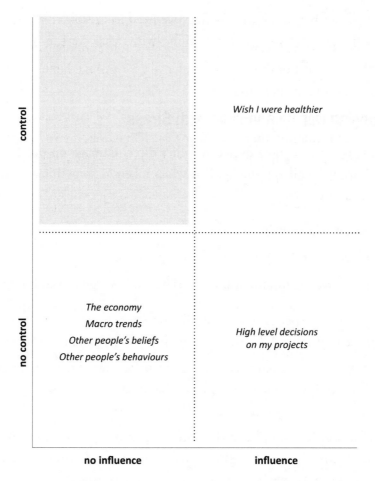

Figure 15.1   Mapping your stressors.

Explaining the Matrix

Control + Influence

The things within your control and influence that are stressing you out are the ones you must take action on, whether that's killing the task, changing the parameters, delegating, etc. You have to create an action plan for everything in this box to decrease the stress surrounding the tasks.

No Control + Influence

The things you can't control but have some influence over you must influence, but then let go – you can't control the outcome, so it's important to recognise that.

Remember, it's your perception of control, or rather lack of control, over a situation that stresses you out. However, if you have never had control in the first place, it's important to acknowledge that you can't dictate the outcome.

Once you've influenced as much as you can, you must let go and accept the outcome for what it is.

No Control + No Influence

For the situations or events stressing you that are both out of your influence and control, you need to adopt a more 'Zen' attitude and really *let go* of the anxiety.

Meditation and mindfulness help create space between stressors and your reaction to them. But allowing something you have neither influence nor control over to affect your emotions, stress levels, and overall well-being is irrational – you must practise and perfect the art of 'letting go'.

Use this tool as a handy exercise any time that you're feeling overwhelmed. The great thing about it is that you can use it to help other people as well, perhaps people that you manage or who are in your team, to deal with their own stress levels and get perspective on what's driving them and what they can do about it.

The statistics on mental wellbeing are beyond shocking to be honest. We have to believe we're in the process of moving to a completely new understanding. Just as we have a physical body, we have a mental body. Like the physical body, the mental body is on a spectrum of healthiness at any given time. Virtually everybody is mentally and physically unwell at some point in their lives. So, equipping people to manage both their mental and physical bodies is the right and natural thing to do.

— *Tim Munden, Chief Learning Officer, Unilever*

Mental fitness is everything. It's the key to productivity. It's the key to enhanced physical activity. It's key in creativity. Strong mental fitness allows your team, your people, to understand, explore and seize opportunity when it comes along. If you're too busy scrambling around at the bottom, just dealing with day-to-day minutia of things going wrong, you're never going to get your head above the clouds to see what possibilities are actually out there. It's mental fitness that helps you do this.

— *Aldo Kane, Adventurer, Record Setter and former Royal Marines Commando*

16 Overcoming the Amygdala Hijack

When it comes to stress, *distraction* has a big role to play. Not all stress is bad, and the best stress focuses our attention – think about that deadline that you suddenly had that made you hyper-focused and productive. Often the key to helping us feel less stressed and more focused is eliminating the unnecessary distractions in our life.

We have two primary distractions: internal distractions and external distractions. We can get pulled in both ways. Let's get into internal distractions and, more importantly, how to manage them.

The biggest internal distractions are our emotions; they are attention magnets, and managing our emotions is vital if we are to have more efficient focus. Daniel Goleman, the author of *Emotional Intelligence and Focus*, states that emotions make us pay attention right now. They grab our attention and tell us, 'This is urgent, focus!'

He also coined the term 'amygdala hijack' (Figure 16.1). I talked previously about how the amygdala can just take over and 'hijack' the prefrontal cortex. This is when it primarily takes all the energy from the prefrontal cortex and demands that you fight, flight, or freeze. It can be immediate and overwhelming, which is why often we find ourselves in a state of confusion.

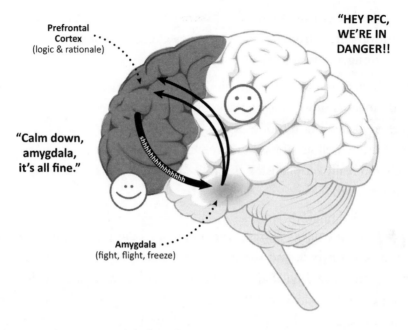

Figure 16.1 Amygdala hijack.

What happens in the brain when you're stressed?

Any time we have a sense of fear, insecurity, doubt, worry, or anxiety, a pathway between our amygdala and our prefrontal cortex gets activated. The amygdala is part of the limbic system, often referred to as the place where the fight, flight, or freeze response occurs.

It's designed to prioritise our survival in any and all situations, like our alarm system when we feel threatened in any way. It's designed to protect us, but sometimes it can be oversensitive.

As I mentioned in Part 3, 'Owning Our Thinking', this neurological bias was designed to ensure our survival from predators. These days, the danger is less likely to be a real physical threat and more likely to be triggered by an email from our boss!

But because the amygdala is the oldest part of our brain, the neural pathways firing from it to the prefrontal cortex (sending panic signals!) are strong and well used.

What's important about the amygdala when it's on high alert is that it shuts down our prefrontal cortex which is at the front of the brain. As a result, not only are you overcome with emotion and panic or fear, as well as stress, but any chance you have of soothing yourself and really rationalising things is taken away when your prefrontal cortex is off.

Even though the predators no longer exist, in the modern world we do have a lot of *congestion*, we have a lot of deadlines, and speed is of the essence. We're living in a very fast-paced world and because of that, we more often than not find ourselves in the amygdala hijack situation. That's why it's so important to be aware of it and to regulate our emotions if we want to have a balanced life.

As I mentioned earlier, neurobiologist Richard Davidson discovered that people who are emotionally resilient and have more of a positive mindset have strong neural pathways *from the prefrontal cortex to the amygdala*. For these people, the negative feelings generated by the amygdala peter out, and they don't get mired in feelings like unhappiness or resentment.

By contrast, people with little emotional resilience have fewer or weaker signals *from their prefrontal cortex to the amygdala*, due to either low activity or poor connections.

The good news is that we can exercise and strengthen our neural pathways through repeated practice. On the next pages, you'll find different exercises and some simple behaviour 'hacks' to strengthen this important pathway, helping to train your brain to prepare for, and positively respond to, negative or challenging situations.

Four Ways to Take Back Your Amygdala

There are four things that you can do.

Meditate

A lot of research has been conducted into the effectiveness of mindfulness, not just in the moment, but its long-term effects too.

Mindfulness-Based Stress Reduction (MBSR) is a healing approach that combines meditation and yoga. Developed by Dr Jon Kabat-Zinn in the 1970s, it aims to address the unconscious thoughts, feelings, and behaviours thought to increase stress and undermine your health. Research backs up the claims of MBSR. One such study[1] measured people's brains using an MRI before and after an eight-week MBSR course. They found that after the eight weeks, the grey matter around the amygdala had reduced and had changed structurally as a result of the mindfulness training. The mindfulness practice had created new neural pathways in the brain.

In another study, they found that 20 minutes of mindfulness a day resulted in a significant difference on attention tests in as little as four days.

This shows you don't need to spend decades meditating or go off to Nepal before you get the benefits. If you're committed, and actually even if you're not, just four days can change your brain. If you haven't already tried it, I really encourage you to do so. There are so many apps out there. Even five minutes a day can start to make a difference.

---

[1] Gotink, R. A., Hermans, K. S., Geschwind, N. et al. (2016) 'Mindfulness and Mood Stimulate Each Other in an Upward Spiral: A Mindful Walking Intervention Using Experience Sampling', *Mindfulness*, 7: 1114–1122.

Counting from 1 to 10

If you're angry, count to ten in your mind before you say anything.
If you are very angry, count to one hundred.

—Thomas Jefferson

It sounds simple, but Jefferson was right. When you count, you are switching 'on' the prefrontal cortex (the part of your brain that deals with logical thinking), which has just been shut off by the amygdala hijacking. Forcing yourself to count 'overrides' the amygdala which has gotten you in the state of fight, flight, or freeze.

If you start to count while you feel that intense emotion, you effectively get some space from it. When you force your mind to do some logical thinking, like counting to 10, counting backwards from 10, or remembering your phone number, for example, it helps a lot.

Counting and Breathing

The sympathetic nervous system is responsible for fight or flight. Then there's the parasympathetic nervous system, which is responsible for rest and digestion.

When you take those deep mindful breaths, you are activating the parasympathetic nervous system, and the net result is that you feel calmer and more focused.

Combine intentional counting with mindful breathing, and you have a surprisingly powerful tool to combat amygdala hijack and regain control.

Close your eyes and focus on the breath. If you begin to think about something else, just gently bring your focus back to the breath.

Don't judge yourself if your mind begins to wander, just return your attention to your breath.

Every time you bring the wandering mind back to this state, you're working the concentration muscle.

If you're ever in a situation at home or at work where you just want to explode or get angry, use this technique. When you are in a highly emotional state, it's the quickest way to gain control of your prefrontal cortex and get your parasympathetic nervous system in action. Count to 10 and with each breath count as well.

Silent Scream

This one is excellent if you find yourself in a situation where you've got a lot of adrenaline pumping through your body. In that moment your eyes will dilate, your voice will start to shake, and your veins will actually move away from being too close to the skin. All of this is preparing you for attack or to be attacked.

Let's take an example. It's like how some people will feel when they have to get on a stage in front of lots of people. They get overcome by emotion and the advice they're often given is, 'Just imagine that the audience are naked.' That does not work; you need to beat physiology with physiology.

The quickest way to get rid of the adrenaline going through your body and deal with the physical effects of the amygdala hijack is to tackle it with physiology.

The Silent Scream is simple and effective.

Go somewhere ideally private (so people don't think you're crazy) and clench your whole body, bend your knees, contract all of your muscles, and scream silently. You can, of course, scream properly as long as you know you aren't going to alarm anyone!

Do this until you're out of air.

When you are in fight/flight mode, you have adrenaline going through your body, and you need to dissipate that adrenaline. Unless you're going to punch someone (which I don't recommend), or go for a run around the building, the best way to get it through and out of your body is by acting as if you are in some sort of intense fight without having to be in one. Once you do this, it will help you to control your heart rate, your voice will return to normal, your breathing will become calmer, and the adrenaline will be released.

Use this exercise in intense situations. But as I said, try not to do it in public, or you will raise some eyebrows. Again, this is another way of really making sure that your focus is on the right things and that you are taking control of your emotions before you make important decisions or take actions. Consider the number of decisions people are making daily at work when under pressure or heightened stress. You can then multiply this figure for more senior staff; the higher up the food chain, the more the demands on people's time, the bigger and riskier decisions need to be taken often with less data or certainly without being as close to the details. If we all started to implement some of these tools, we'd be able to distance ourselves from the emotional charge, create some 'headspace', and make more considered choices. What would that be worth to your company? What would be the compound impact if everyone in your business collectively learned how to make decisions under stress but without experiencing its direct negative impact?

It's easy to think this is just about wellbeing and mental health, but it's really about all of the good things that we want for mankind and humanity, for our societies and for our businesses. These things can only come to fruition through human beings, so we want human beings to be both highly developed and thriving. It's about how much we are really helping them to access their capabilities and then how well a person is. Wellness and performance are linked, but they're also distinct. You can be a very developed human being, but then succumb to a mental illness, so I think we have to work across the two dimensions to truly get results.

– *Tim Munden, Chief Learning Officer, Unilever*

There are so many different parts that you can use that will ultimately make your team not just perform as a team, but perform at an elite level. The Royal Marines are an elite fighting force and we operate at the highest functioning level that you can operate at. That comes down to lots of different things, but all of that is directly transferable into business and that winning mental fitness edge can be trained, it can be practiced and it can even be fun.

– *Aldo Kane, Adventurer, Record Setter and former Royal Marines Commando*

17 Flow Versus Frazzle

I've just been talking to you about the biggest internal distractions of all, which are our emotions. When you're in a heightened emotional state, we're actually talking about stress. Stress can be very distracting from our focus, but we're also talking about performance, because what do you need focus for? To achieve whatever your goals might be for that day or for your life.

The relationship between stress and performance has been well known in psychology for over a century. It's called the Yerkes–Dodson Law.[1] Yerkes and Dodson didn't actually know that this was what they were looking at, at the time. It is only with hindsight that we recognise what they had uncovered. It's a very different way of thinking about how the brain operates, but the term 'flow' has made its way into day-to-day conversations.

On the bell chart below (Figure 17.1), you can see that flow is in the middle. Before flow we've got disengagement, and frazzle is on the other side. These may be terms that you haven't heard of before. Daniel Goleman said, *'Each of these has a powerful impact on a person's*

[1]Dodson, J. D. and Yerkes, R. M. (1908) 'The Relation of Strength of Stimulus to Rapidity of Habit-Formation', *Journal of Comparative Neurology and Psychology*, 18: 459–482.

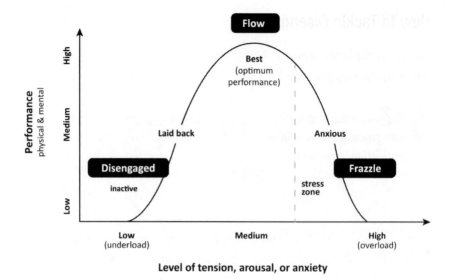

Figure 17.1   The Yerkes–Dodson curve.

ability to perform at their best, disengagement and frazzle torpedo our efforts while flow lets them soar'.[2]

The three main states are Disengaged, Flow, and Frazzle:

> Disengaged: When people are bored, you see randomly scattered neural activation, rather than a sharp delineation of activity in the areas relevant to the task.

> Flow: When people are in flow, only those brain areas relevant to the activity at hand are activated.

> Frazzle: When people are stressed, you find lots of activity in the emotional circuitry that is irrelevant to the task at hand, and which suggests a state of anxious distractedness.

---

[2]Goleman, D. (2012) 'The Sweet Spot for Achievement', *Psychology Today* <https://www.psychologytoday.com/intl/blog/the-brain-and-emotional-intelligence/201203/the-sweet-spot-achievement>

How to Tackle Disengagement

Many workplaces around the world have varying numbers of people stuck in disengagement: bored, uninspired, and disinterested.

> *The good news is that the scientists who've been studying motivation have given us a new approach. It's built much more around intrinsic motivation. Around the desire to do things because they matter, because we like it.*
>
> —Daniel Pink, TED Talk The Puzzle of Motivation

Motivation often comes from finding a personal purpose or goal within the work that we do. Answering the questions:

- What can I uniquely bring to this project that will improve it in some way?
- What can I focus on that will not only get the business/project results but will be personally fulfilling and rewarding for me also?

We have run countless numbers of purpose workshops for our clients over the years. These are focused on helping people uncover what drives and motivates them, what impact they want to have in the world, and what skills they can contribute. They can be profound sessions and are as rewarding for me to run as they can be for others to participate in. Much research[3] has now been conducted on the role of personal purpose and its impact on productivity and well-being:

- Business experts make the case that purpose is a key to exceptional performance.
- Psychologists describe it as the pathway to greater well-being.
- Doctors have even found that people with purpose in their lives are less prone to disease.

---

[3]Craig, N. and Snook S. A. (2014, May) 'From Purpose to Impact', *Harvard Business Review* <https://hbr.org/2014/05/from-purpose-to-impact>

Having a purpose within a project matters; having goals we are motivated by matters. Deep down, we all want significance, and knowing that our work matters goes a long way in enhancing an individual's mental fitness. I have much to say on the topic of purpose, but that's a book in itself.

What Happens During 'Frazzle'?

The neurobiology of frazzle is the same for panic and fear – the amygdala hijack.

When demands become too great for us to handle, when we get overwhelmed and have a sense of too much to do, our brain secretes too many stress hormones that interfere with our ability to focus.

We shut down, we can no longer work well, learn, innovate, listen, or plan effectively. When we are feeling frazzled, it's important to step away from whatever we are doing, take a break, get some rest, or go outside for a change of scene.

If we're overwhelmed by the magnitude of a task, the best thing to do is break it down into all of its component parts. Below is a simple but helpful exercise for managing overwhelm.

Get some Post-It® notes, and write down as many tasks as possible, one per Post-It® note. Once you have it all out of your head, then organise the tasks, either simply in terms of what needs to happen first (stick them on a wall for visibility) or in themed groups (e.g. admin tasks versus strategic thinking). Once you have mapped out all of the tasks, make a plan for how you can get everything done. Ask yourself these three questions:

- Do I have the capacity to do all of these tasks?
    - If yes, then plan what needs to happen first.
    - If no, work out what you can delegate or who you can bring in to help you.
- Do I have the time?

- If yes, put in order of priority.
- If no, see which tasks you can renegotiate timelines on.
  - If none, see what you can delegate, outsource, etc.
- Do I have the capability?
  - If yes, put in order of priority as above.
  - If no, see who you can bring in to help.

What Happens When We're in 'Flow'?

Where we want to be on the Yerkes–Dodson arc is the zone of optimal performance, known as 'flow'.

Flow represents a peak of self-regulation, and maximum performance or learning.

A little bit of stress is actually good for us. It gets us motivated and out of the disengaged zone and into the flow zone. That might show up for you as a deadline or a phone call from your boss. Sometimes we will allow ourselves to be disengaged until a deadline creates a sense of urgency. Stress isn't always bad, and it is good to feel a little bit of it, but just not too much.

We can enhance our ability to get into flow by 'preparing the stage'. That means creating the right environment for optimal performance. For example:

- Get the basics right – Get a good night's sleep, eat, and perhaps exercise.
  - This will lessen internal distractions.
- Pre-empt distractions – Clear your diary, turn off all notifications on your computer and your phone.
  - This will lessen external distractions.
- If you work well with music, choose the album best suited to the type of work you'll be doing.

- Prepare for future distractions – Have snacks and refreshments at hand. Have everything you need already at hand (so you don't go on a one-hour escapade looking for paper!).

Being in flow is very satisfying; it's a great mix of progress and fulfilment.

Mihaly Csikszentmihalyi (University of Chicago)[4] describes flow as the state in which people are so immersed in what they're doing that their brain simply can't focus on anything else.

What's interesting is that he really understood that getting in flow is a *perfect combination between ability (and skill level) and challenge.* So, if the challenge is low and your skill is high – and you've seen this with very smart kids in the classrooms – you'll be bored. If the challenge is high and your skill is low, you'll be in a frazzle and stressed out; you'll be in a state of anxiety. Therefore, you want to find the perfect balance between having some skill and a challenge that is actually a bit of a stretch, but not an over-stretch. This is when we are at our best in terms of performance.

Stress and Mindset

Research[5] has found that we tend to have one of two stress mindsets: a stress-is-enhancing mindset (SEM) or a stress-is-debilitating mindset (SDM). The way we experience stress is dependent on which of these mindsets we adopt.

In simple terms, if you have an SEM, you believe stress enhances performance, productivity, health and well-being, learning, and

---

[4] Csikszentmihályi, M. (1990) *Flow: The Psychology of Optimal Experience*, Harper & Row, ISBN 978-0-06-016253-5

[5] Crum, A. J., Salovey, P., and Achor, S. (2013). 'Rethinking Stress: The Role of Mindsets in Determining the Stress Response', *Journal of Personality and Social Psychology*, 104 (4): 716 in How to reduce stress by changing mindset research briefing', Research Briefing. *The Oxford Review.* <www.oxford-review.com>

growing; and if you have an SDM, you believe stress is detrimental in these areas. These mindsets are either/or. There is no in between.

The good news is that you can change your stress mindset. Research conducted on mindsets[6] in general has shown that, with the right intervention, it's possible to change your mindset relatively quickly.

Where stress is concerned, this can significantly reduce the negative impact it has.

A 2019 study[7] using electroencephalography (EEG) recording techniques of the brain's electrical activity and cortisol levels found that changing your stress mindset has an almost immediate positive impact on the mind and body's experience of stress. This means it's possible for stress to be used positively rather than negatively by simply changing your mindset.

Stress and Your Health

One study[8] tracked 30 000 adults in the United States for eight years, and they started by asking people how much stress they experienced in the last year. They also asked if they believed that stress is harmful for their health. Then they used public death records to find out who died.

People who experienced a lot of stress in the previous year and viewed stress as harmful had a 43% increased risk of dying. People who experienced a lot of stress but did not view stress as harmful were no more likely to die. In fact, they had the lowest risk of dying of anyone in the study, including people who had relatively little stress.

---

[6]Dweck, C. (2006) *Mindset: The New Psychology of Success*, New York, NY: Random House.
[7]Park, H. and Hahm, S. (2019) 'Changes in Stress Mindset and EEG through E-Healthcare Based Education', *IEEE Access*, 7: 20163–20171.
[8]Keller, A., Litzelman, K., and Wisk, L. E. (2012) 'Does the Perception That Stress Affects Health Matter? The Association with Health and Mortality', *Health Psychology*, 31: 677–684 - PMC - PubMed

The researchers estimated that over the eight years they were tracking deaths, 182 000 Americans died prematurely, not from stress but from the belief that stress is bad for you.

As the stress researcher Kelly McGonnigal points out:

'That is over 20 000 deaths a year. Now, if that estimate is correct, that would make believing stress is bad for you the 15th largest cause of death in the United States last year, killing more people than skin cancer, HIV AIDS and homicide'.

The study raised the question – can changing how you think about stress make you healthier?

To test this hypothesis, an experiment was run where they taught people to reframe their typical stress response as helpful instead of being a sign of something 'bad' (Figure 17.2).

That pounding heart is preparing you for action. If you're breathing faster it's good, it's getting more oxygen to your brain. Participants who learned to view the stress response as helpful for their performance were less stressed, less anxious, and more confident.

When reviewing this study, Dr McGonnigal pointed out that the most fascinating finding was how the participants' physical stress response changed. In a typical stress response, your heart rate

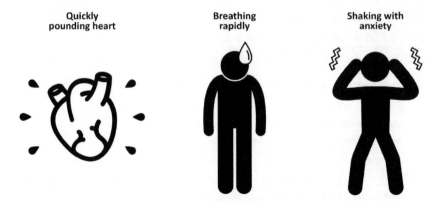

Figure 17.2   Stress response.

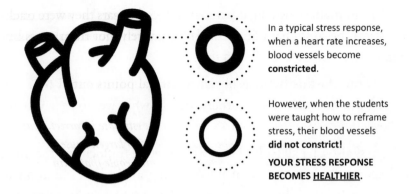

In a typical stress response, when a heart rate increases, blood vessels become **constricted**.

However, when the students were taught how to reframe stress, their blood vessels **did not constrict!**
YOUR STRESS RESPONSE BECOMES <u>HEALTHIER</u>.

Figure 17.3   How stress affects the heart.

goes up and your blood vessels constrict – one of the reasons that chronic stress is sometimes associated with cardiovascular disease (Figure 17.3).

But in the study, when participants viewed their stress response as helpful, their blood vessels stayed relaxed. Their heart was still pounding, but it demonstrated a much healthier cardiovascular profile. It actually looks a lot like what happens in moments of joy and courage. Over a lifetime of stressful experiences, this one biological change could be the difference between a stress-induced heart attack at the age of 50 and living well into your 90s. Therefore, the *new science of stress reveals that how you think about stress matters.*

As Dr McGonnigal goes on to say:

When you choose to view your stress response as helpful, you create the biology of courage. And when you choose to connect with others under stress, you can create resilience. Now, I wouldn't necessarily ask for more stressful experiences in my life. But the science has given me a whole new appreciation for stress. Stress gives us access to our hearts; the compassionate heart that finds joy and meaning in connecting with others, and yes, your pounding physical heart, working so hard to give you strength and energy. When you choose to view stress in this way, you're not just getting better at stress, you're actually making a pretty profound statement. You're saying that you can trust yourself to handle life's challenges.

To summarise, we all get stressed in life. The goal is not to eradicate stress (because that's impossible) but to manage our relationship with it.

We can do this by focusing on what we have control over and putting our attention there rather than on what we don't have control over.

Stress also isn't all bad: a bit of stress is good for focusing the mind and getting us into a state of flow, as long as we have the tools to manage it. In the following few pages, I've given you a 'stress toolkit' which you can dip into and out of when you need it.

Managing Stress: In the Moment

When you're feeling overwhelmed and need a mental break to reboot or refresh your brain, or you're feeling anxious, nervous or stressed about something or someone, consider these quick easy methods to get yourself back on track.

- **If you're in conflict with someone**, first, don't judge the other person, because you don't know what else might be contributing to the tension outside of the situation. Next, take a deep breath and demonstrate openness by helping them verbalise their needs and encouraging them to share. You can ask questions like:
  - 'Where is your uncertainty coming from?'
  - 'What can I do to help you right now?'
  - 'Tell me more about why you're feeling that'.

Above all, *listen* to what they're saying instead of planning your response. You can and should also ask for the same courtesy when it's your turn to speak.

- **Breathing (4-6-8 Technique)**. First, breathe in and exhale through your mouth, making a whoosh sound. Next, inhale quietly through your nose for a count of 4. Hold your breath for a count of 6, then exhale completely through your mouth, making a whoosh sound to a count of 8. Repeat five times. This rhythmic breathing well help bring your heart back to its normal rhythm (a consistent pattern) and will also help bring your prefrontal cortex back online if you're experiencing amygdala hijack).

- **Walk away.** This doesn't mean *run* away or ignore the situation; this means give yourself at least five minutes to remove yourself from an escalating situation before it gets out of hand. If you are in an argument with someone, politely say you need X amount of time and you will promise to come back to them then.

- **555.** Sit down and take a minute or two to observe your surroundings (indoors or outdoors). In your head, take note of 5 visuals, 5 sounds, 5 feelings or sensations. Pause long enough to connect to each of the five visuals, sounds, and feelings. Really absorb the senses and notice how the mind begins to settle in the present.

- **Ask yourself why?** Why exactly are you feeling stressed? Have you done everything you could to help the situation? If the control of the situation is out of your hands, and you cannot do more, is there a reason for being stressed? If you need help, what specifically can someone help you with, and do you know who you can ask for it?

Tracking your stress response

It's important to be aware of what happens to you internally when you experience stress. Having this awareness will enable you to recognise the signs and head them off before you enter a typical stress response.

Think about the last stressful situation you were in and answer the questions below. This will help you to start

(continued)

(continued)

recognising your typical stress responses so you can tune into them and have a better chance of controlling your reaction.

1. Briefly describe what happened.

2. What sensations did you experience in your body? Where?

3. What thoughts did you have?

4. What did you do, and has this happened before?

5. What can you do differently next time?

Managing Stress: At Work

In nearly every second of every day we are bombarded with input from our external and internal worlds. We are forced to process and multitask at an alarming rate and are often attempting to put out fire after fire. While productivity is important, equally important is the need to give your mind proper rest to recharge, recentre, and work out thoughts and ideas. The following are simple behavioural 'hacks' to help you begin to manage and control your environment and thus your relationship with stress.

At work:

- **Don't start the day with email;** instead check your emails at 10 am, and use the time before to write down your three core objectives for the day and the plan to implement and work on them.

- **Accept all meetings you are invited to** but only join the ones with clear objectives that you can actively contribute to. Don't shy away from asking for an agenda and objectives, and if you can share info via email instead, do that.

- **Do not eat lunch at your desk;** if you do, it should be an *exception* (max. once per week). It's important to give yourself and your mind a rest. Even if it's just a short 30 minutes, sit or walk with a colleague to get lunch. This is not a marathon, you can take a break!

- **When working on a project that requires deep concentration**, consider setting an out-of-office reply explaining that you're work- ing on a big project and will only be checking emails at 10 am and 2 pm for the next X days. For anything urgent, refer them to your communication channel of choice. You may still get unnec- essary messages, but at the very least people will think twice before contacting you!

- **Break it down.** A project can seem overwhelming when looked at as a whole. Breaking it down and into milestones and manageable

steps makes it easier to reach your goals. Use Post-It® notes to map
your project milestones out on your office wall!

- **Delegate, postpone, eliminate.** Assess each task on your list by
  asking:
  - Is the task important to you/the business?
  - Will it relieve pressure?
  - Is it 'on strategy'?
  - Can it be done only by you?
  - Does it help you move forward?

    If not, check if you can delegate, postpone, or eliminate the
  task completely. See the table on the next page to help you.

- **Remind yourself of the 'bigger picture'.** To ensure the greatest
  output of your energy, understand the bigger purpose of the task.
  It's easy to get tunnel vision and burn energy on small tasks, but
  progress on things that do not ladder up to the bigger picture are
  just distractions. Always check in with how what you're about to
  do relates to the bigger picture.

Assessing your task list

Another quick and easy trick is to filter your tasks. Fill in the
following table to help you assess your tasks, break them down
into manageable chunks, and prioritise them effectively. Once
you've filled it in, review and make a decision about what needs
to get done first and what can be done by someone else.

Task	Is it important to you or the business?	Is it 'on strategy'?	Can it *only* be done by you?	Does it help you move forward?	Delegate, postpone or eliminate?

Managing Stress: At Home

Setting boundaries around your home or personal time is important. Work is only a part (albeit a big one) of the overall scheme of life, and home is the space where you can explore and work on the *other* things that can bring great reward and satisfaction, like your well-being and health, personal goals, family, interests, hobbies, etc.

At home:

- **Mindfulness apps** improve your ability to remain calm under pressure. A daily 10-minute practice can increase flexibility, adaptability, creativity, and focus. Suggested apps: Headspace & Calm.

- **Decide what time you officially go offline** and switch off *all* phone/messaging notifications on your phone. You should also let your colleagues know that after X time they should not expect a response. If you still get messages, ignore them; you need to protect this mental space for yourself.

- **Do not send emails after 6 pm or at weekends.** Even if you have to work, keep your inbox set to 'offline' – sending emails might feel productive, but they could stress out others or signal that they can start emailing you. Set your boundaries and commit to them.

- **Break the screen addiction.** Yes, this is an obvious one, but also one that's so easy to get drawn into when you're 'bored' waiting in line at the store, waking up in the morning, or winding down after (or even during!) dinner. There are several apps to help fight, limit, or block social media, like Offtime, Moment, Flipd, or Space to name a few. If you prefer less involved methods:

  - Use airplane mode or turn off your notifications and put your phone in another room during important moments like dinner with your family.

  - Make it harder to access your phone and apps by setting a very long passcode.

  - Set a rule at home: No phones/screens between or after the hours of X – and stick to it!

    As a minimum, don't use any form of technology at least one hour before sleep – this will increase the quality of your night's rest.

- **Don't charge your phone, laptop, or tablet in your bedroom.** You may be tempted to 'quickly check' your email or get sucked into an Instagram blackhole if your phone is within easy reach.

If you use your phone for an alarm, buy an old-fashioned alarm clock!

- **Define your 'self-care strategy'.** Think about the following categories: Basic, Emotional, Relationships, and Physical. Use the table on the following page to write down things for each that help you relax and feel 'okay' again – this will be your go-to list for making sure you're taking care of your needs. When you start to feel stressed, refer to the list to choose an activity to help lower your stress levels.

For example:

- Basic – eating a delicious meal, drinking enough water, getting eight hours of uninterrupted sleep.
- Emotional – writing in my journal.
- Relationships – weekly contact with mom (even if it's just a quick text), quiet dinner with my husband.
- Physical – time in nature, walking, yoga, listening to my favourite band.

My self-care strategy

Use the following template to define your self-care strategy.

Basic	Emotional
Relationships	**Physical**

We've given you stress toolkit so that you have a variety of ways of managing moments where you feel stressed or overwhelmed. Even those who've been practicing and strengthening their mental fitness still experience stress; no one is immune. That's why it's important to know what you can do both in those moments and in preparation for those moments. The more we practice, just like training our muscles in the gym, the stronger our neural pathways will be. So, when the unexpected happens, we already have the right habits in place to navigate them with ease.

It's simple, people just want to work for an organisation that looks after them, especially now ... You've got to look at those successful organisations in the time of crisis. They've been successful because their people are engaged, they want to be there and, in part, some of that is about purpose and wellbeing but a lot of it is about engagement. Those threads of being engaged are about you being attracted or wanting to continue to work for an organisation because the company cares for you, or because someone within the organisation has done something for you, to make you engage and go the extra mile, so now you want to return it. And if you trace a lot of those threads back, a lot of it is about being supported and connected to purpose or having a strong wellbeing proposition. It's about a healthy relationship between organisation and employee; a mutual respect, mutual support and mutual wellbeing.

– *Marcus Hunt, Head of Global Health Services, EMEA,*
Johnson & Johnson

It's applicable to everyone. We're talking about things that make your life more effective, more productive, more joyous and more many things. But for me the thing that is really important is the positive impact of this. It's unlocking a potential. It's the idea of creating the presence of positives not the absence of negatives that makes me most motivated by it.

— Shawn Conway, CEO, Peet's Coffee

MENTAL FITNESS IN PRACTICE

Unilever: A Case Study

Hopefully, you have been applying what you've learned in this book to yourself and your own professional development, but how does it all fit into a wider team and corporate environment? We've brought Mental Fitness into Unilever, Jacobs Douwe Egberts, Coca-Cola and many others. Whilst that might create creditability, I think it's more important for people to hear about the *impact* mental fitness training has had on the people who have experienced it. Because of the nature of our work, much of what we do is confidential. However, we do have permission from Unilever to share the following case study which illustrates not only how we can share these valuable concepts and learnings on a much larger scale, but more importantly the significant benefits of doing so.

Unilever is a global FMCG company that owns more than 400 brands and employs more than 155 000 people in 190 countries.

In the past 10 years, Unilever has initiated multiple major organisational restructures in order to remain relevant, operationally strong, and agile in the new world. One global Unilever function in particular, CMI (Consumer & Market Insights), has redesigned itself in a number of ways to maximise expertise while continuing to support brand teams with market and consumer insight.

As with all major redesigns, there have been both benefits and consequences. That's why it's essential to have ongoing programmes in place after the initial change, to manage the expected and unexpected consequences of such redesigns.

We supported Unilever's global CMI function to do just that, as well as:

- Successfully work through the organisational restructure while **avoiding the usual drop in customer satisfaction**, where a 24% *drop* in customer satisfaction and a 22% *reduction* in loyalty is typical.

- **Shorten the time it usually takes for junior staff to gain the corporate experience** required to find their voice and footing in an intense, rapidly changing environment to confidently collaborate with senior leaders and implement change in a complex organisation.

- Create an environment where **77% of participants claimed an increase in performance and increased their overall motivation by 15%.**

- **Positively affect the resilience and mental fitness of 86%** of participating team members, an issue that is now top of mind with many corporations struggling with the current crisis caused by the global pandemic and the ongoing changes to business they will need to endure in order to stay relevant.

Key challenges for Unilever

Challenge #1: Minimising disruption and reducing tension and pressure in the workplace No company is immune to change in a global marketplace that's hyper-focused on improving key performance indicators (KPIs). The life expectancy of a Fortune 500 firm in the 1960s was around 61 years. Today it's less than 18 years. Uncertainty, speed of change, changing consumer and customer expectations, and digital disruption all pose new questions and require organisations, leaders, and teams to adapt and evolve to stay relevant.

Companies facing budget restrictions, or those looking to implement new business strategies, find that these initiatives often require new leadership, relocations, tighter budgets, and workload increases for junior staff to ensure that company goals are being met.

Unilever, as a whole, was in the middle of a restructuring process that involved changing roles, the formation of new teams, people leaving the company, and the hiring of new talent. While this process isn't new to the company, integrating team members after these changes brought complexity.

Knowing that CMI is a critical and highly valued function within the business, the CMI Leadership Team needed a solution that would minimise disruption, reduce tension and pressure with internal business partners, and improve motivation and communication within their teams. They needed a solution before job satisfaction and employee morale was negatively impacted.

Challenge #2: Rapidly creating an integrated, high-functioning workforce In addition to the restructure, other factors had stirred up tension as employees strived to change their old ways of working for new. Business partners also had to adjust their expectations and the assumed deliverables of each team within the function.

To meet these increased business demands, improve team collaboration, productivity, and elevate the function overall, CMI focused on enhancing the skills of 300 people over a two-year period. No small undertaking, but a demonstration of their commitment to positive change.

Some of the issues the teams were facing included:

1. *Tension at every level:* Company and function-wide communication from senior leadership not landing in the intended way, or landing too late, bred some feelings of frustration, and general unrest. Communication and misaligned expectations (or unmet expectations) are common issues in most restructures, but important to address nonetheless.

2. *Increased pressure to deliver:* A demand to increase performance and deliverables while not increasing costs – an ambitious target – and one which stretched already thin resources.

3. *Steep learning curve:* The need to quickly onboard new employees in companies can sometimes increase the organisational learning curve, resulting in employees feeling lost or unsure of their place and hesitant to speak up and engage until they feel they know or understand more.

4. *Lack of organisational clarity:* Role shuffling, and lack of clarity regarding roles and responsibilities, left existing employees feeling confused and concerned. This led to some territorial behaviours and a general low-level frustration around a perceived imbalance of labour.

Challenge #3: Accelerating the organisational learning curve Particularly in junior work levels or those new to a company, a lack of confidence and organisational knowledge, typically developed and practised over the course of a career, can affect productivity and the overall impact of a team or function.

Unilever experienced this first-hand.

In this case, the company had the global reach to attract new and fresh talent and specialists from various industries, including start-ups, but many found the speed of settling in challenging. When joining any big corporate as a junior it can take some time to navigate the structure and politics, which can leave some people feeling unsure of themselves.

This led to many not 'speaking up' when required to give inputs, or not engaging with business partners or senior leaders from a position of authority, as they lacked the overall confidence which usually comes with time.

As one director put it: *'They need to make themselves wanted at the table, not just add to the number of people in a meeting.'*

> This was such a good journey for me –a reminder on our cognitive filters (i.e. the way we see the world) and how this can truly impact our work and our interactions. That we need to consciously decide how to deal with difficult/tricky situations that we do not have control over. The second learning for me was on my self-imposed limitations and how to consciously challenge myself to not only overcome but to exceed my own expectations.
>
> *– Programme participant, Unilever*

Challenge #4: Creating and rolling out a cost-effective, yet impactful, global development plan

When rolling out any global initiatives, there are always issues of time, location, and logistics.

In today's competitive marketplace, large corporations are forced to maximise time as much as possible. In CMI's case, there was a need to rapidly provide a programme for 300 people across 26 countries and multiple time zones, potentially rolling it out to other functions across the globe.

Global training initiatives can often face logistical and cost challenges in scaling programmes where vendors need to be physically present to deliver content, or deliver through a 'train the trainer' approach where internal HR has to be trained on content and facilitation skills. From a global perspective, neither of these options is ideal, as they could add time, cost, and resource to the initiative.

Because of this and the impact of the global pandemic, many corporations have embraced online learning programmes as they offer flexibility in scheduling, are often more cost-effective to implement, allow companies to track performance and engagement, and make it easier for them to identify and learn from employee outcomes.

Translating face-to-face experiences

Although there are many benefits to virtual, where some suppliers fall short is in simply translating existing face-to-face programmes to online. This opens up a different set of hurdles to overcome. In a virtual world, special attention needs to be paid to the following to create change that is truly impactful:

- Building trust and rapport between participants and the facilitators, which is particularly important for longer programmes
- Having the right balance and mix of content delivery (live, self-serve, etc.)
- Solidifying learning for practical applications
- Ensuring employees are engaged and feel supported
- Fostering a sense of community and shared learning

In addition, since there is a considerable upfront effort and investment for the provider in creating engaging virtual experiences, most programmes or content tend to be standardised and 'off the shelf', which doesn't always satisfy client needs.

The solution

Finding Your North: a bespoke solution for development and growth

After working closely with Unilever's CMI team to ensure that the right topics and content were developed in the right way, the result was Finding Your North: a 12-month bespoke programme designed to help individuals accelerate the development of their personal presence and impact. Whilst our mental fitness initiatives can start with 90-minute sessions and one-day intensives, given the scale of what we were trying to achieve and the desire for lasting behaviour change, a 12-month supportive programme met the needs of this particular brief.

Our approach centred around using emotional and social intelligence-based content to help some 300 of CMI's people, who were spread around the world, to increase their mental fitness by really understanding their own thoughts, emotions, and behaviours, and impact these have on their confidence, their interactions with others and the decisions they make on behalf of the business. Not only did they *understand* these, but they also got to regularly apply and practice the techniques to their day jobs. The insights, self-awareness and self-regulation cultivated were what helped participants to embrace change and effectively manage their emotions, ambitions, and behaviour in the face of setbacks and uncertainty.

> This programme teaching social and emotional intelligence couldn't have come at a better time. It has really given people security in their roles, and to make them more valuable in the workplace.
>
> – *Sam Paterson, CMI Gym Project Lead, Unilever*

Being able to scale learning globally, while providing guidance and relevant teaching for each particpant, made it important to run Finding Your North 100% virtually (this was in a pre-COVID world). This ensured that every participant around the world had the same experience, while keeping the individual's needs central to the content.

The programme was split into three phases, each one designed to build upon the insights and learnings of the previous phase. Content was delivered via a blended approach of a 360 emotional and social intelligence assessment, live virtual mini-workshop sessions (variety of topics covered), self-led virtual learning, group and one-to-one coaching sessions and peer mentoring, to cover different learning needs.

Phase 1: Foundations of Self-Awareness

Assessing key challenges and training needs through interviews and surveys, and laying the foundation for change through individual emotional and social intelligence assessment.

Phase 2: Personal Development (Mental Fitness)

Centred around our five-module online mental fitness training course, participants had full access to videos, demos, and PDF downloads to work on developing their cognitive control and self-regulation skills. Further support was provided via live Q&A sessions with me and multiple check-in webinars scheduled throughout the course.

Phase 3: Professional Development (Influence and Impact at Work)

A series of live interactive learning webinar sessions covering a variety of topics designed to cultivate social awareness and relationship management skills, and allow participants to see and apply theory in practical real-life scenarios.

When theory isn't put into practice, valuable lessons can fail to translate into the workplace or towards long-term behaviour change. Phase 3 was essential for teaching participants how to put together and consolidate the learning from Phases 1 and 2, and practise these newly learned skills to become more confident, higher-performing members of the Unilever CMI community.

Below are examples of some of the topics covered in this phase over the two years the programme ran:

- Confidence under pressure
- Effectively managing conflict
- Problem reframing
- Navigating uncertainty
- Motivation and productivity

- Setting boundaries and priority setting
- Energy for performance
- Inspirational leadership

> I can feel the baggage I've been carrying around since child-hood being shrugged off. I feel lighter in spirit, able to choose my response to situations, and more confident and happier in my role. I'm a better business partner because of it.
>
> – *Karen Sears, Director, Global Consumer Insights, Unilever*

The outcome

Big impact, small investment

The results speak for themselves:

- 77% agree that the programme has helped them improve their performance in their job.
- 79% of respondents claim to have more confidence as a result of the programme.
- 80% of respondents believe the investment the business has made has been valuable both to themselves and the business.
- 88% of respondents feel very or extremely motivated in their role (a 15% increase from the programme start).
- 86% of respondents feel well or very well equipped to handle pressure and stress (a 26% increase from the programme start).

Overall positive impact Following the close of the Year 1 pilot programme, the Unilever CMI team saw such a positive impact that they immediately renewed the programme for a second year with an additional 150 participants.

Unilever's CMI participants overwhelmingly bought into the programme, with 85% of respondents saying that the mental fitness course concepts were valuable and easy to use.

Other direct employee testimonials highlighted the programme's effectiveness at helping them identify and overcome workplace obstacles, and develop new methods to become more productive and confident.

> In every module there was something for everyone and feedback was always positive. 'Mental Fitness' has helped participants to truly discover what makes them tick, what drives them, what doesn't and what they can do about it. But it didn't stop there, participants were provided strategies on how to best develop their own strengths, to challenge their weaknesses and to be a substantial player in the world of self-management.
>
> – *Sam Paterson, CMI Gym Project Lead, Unilever*

A combination of factors contributing to a successful experience

The ease of access to content (in addition to the self-guided online course, webinars, and sessions which were available both live and recorded) required an average of one hour of employees' time each two weeks. There was no daily training or hours of meetings required, which minimised any negative effect on productivity.

The programme's engagement tactics, like peer support groups, engagement boards, a points system, etc. were used to build momentum, encourage participants, and impart a sense of accomplishment and growth. This, coupled with the personalised, empathetic attention of our facilitation team, transformed learning from that of a one-way training to a united community experience.

Unilever's perspective The following is a selection of comments from Unilever employees who were involved in the Finding Your North programme:

> *'The programme was developed to help our less experienced team members advance. They need to make themselves wanted at the table, not just add to the number of people in a meeting.'*

> *'In Phase 2, we started the mental fitness course and this is where things got really interesting. It consisted of online modules mixed with a perfect blend of videos, downloads, examples, tutorials and exercises. It was uncomfortably confronting at times which is the space where self-awareness is best nurtured.'*

> *'Having completed the mental fitness course, the biggest change I have noticed in my team is their confidence in themselves. It not only made us more aware of the factors that can hold us back as individuals and the reasons behind that but it gave us the tools to deal with these factors which ultimately results in a more positive and confident team. This course also enabled the team to be far more open in sharing work and asking for support and/or feedback which in turn results in a stronger impact in the business.'*

> *'This was such a good journey for me – a reminder of our cognitive filters (i.e. the way we see the world) and how this can truly impact our work and our interactions. That we need to consciously decide how to deal with difficult/tricky situations that we do not have control over. The second learning for me was on my self-imposed limitations and how to consciously challenge myself to not only overcome but to exceed my own expectations.'*

> *'Thank you to Jodie and everyone behind Finding Your North. The mental fitness course has been personally enriching. The exercises and the reflections are not just about gaining self-confidence but more importantly it gave me back ME.'*

> *'Rather than getting easily offended or taking things personally, I'm thinking more about the reasons I am reacting a certain way and thinking more about where people are coming from.'*

There are many ways to bring mental fitness into your business or team. From short, sharp 90-minute live sessions all the way to more immersive longer-term programmes. Yes, we work with large companies, but we also work with start-ups and small teams. This message is too important to limit access to. The vision at Symbia is to positively impact the lives of 1 million people over the next 3 years and we're on track to do that. If you're interested in learning more, visit us at www.symbiapartners.com or email team@symbiapartners.com.

CONCLUSION

In writing this book, I had two key objectives, the first of which was to help you, the reader, understand what mental fitness is, why it matters, and the importance of bringing it into our businesses as a competitive advantage. This is really what the first third of the book is about.

I also wanted to make your life easier by making the arguments for the case for mental fitness. If you feel inspired after reading this book and want to bring this argument and focus into your business, you have the business case for the benefits of focusing on mental fitness laid out in the initial chapters. If you would like a more detailed business case, you can download one from www.symbiapartners.com/mentalfitnessresources.

The second, and bigger, objective of writing this book was to give you a proper taste of what mental fitness is, what it means for you and your life, and how you can apply it as a practice in your day to day. I've covered the foundations of mental fitness throughout this book, beginning with perception.

Starting with perception was very deliberate, because this is the gateway between our internal and external worlds. The key insight I wanted you to take away from this chapter is that we do not see the world as it is, we see the world as we are. Our interpretation of what goes on around us is open to biases and subjectivity, so if you can accept that your version of events in life is an interpretation, then it must also be true that there are alternative perspectives and interpretations.

Once you accept this, the key is to open your mind to be able to see other perspectives before 'reacting' and instead be able to 'respond'. The chapters on meaning and thinking build on the idea I introduced in the perception chapter, that nothing has inherent meaning, only the meaning that we give to it. We overlay a narrative on our lives. Sometimes it can be good and propel us forwards, and sometimes it can be 'limiting', which will hold us back and keep us down. The aim of these chapters was to raise your awareness of the narrative you overlay onto life and help you understand that you have much more control over it than you may think. You have the ability to shape and adjust that narrative so that it is working for you, not against you.

There is a misconception that we, as humans, are rational, logical thinkers who have emotions, when the reality is that we are emotional beings who also have thoughts, and we tend to attend to our thinking much more than to our emotions.

The chapter about thinking is there to help you tune into your typical thought patterns and mind chatter, and to help you identify whether it's positive and will move you towards a growth mindset and growth thinking, or whether it's limiting and therefore holding you back.

If you remember the mind-body connection, you can see how your thinking can create a chain reaction within you. Your thinking impacts how you feel, which impacts what you do; your emotions impact what you do, which impacts your thoughts; your actions impact your emotions, which also impact your thoughts. I wanted to help you understand this virtuous triangle and demystify each corner of it so you can 'hack' it to your advantage.

I introduced you to new language around thinking traps to help you label your thought patterns in a more coherent way so that you can recognise them, call them out, and adjust your thinking where necessary.

From here I went a level deeper and explored beliefs. These are the underlying scripts of your life, where you have made up rules about your abilities, about your future, and about other people, for better or worse. These rules are usually centred around your capabilities and potential, as well as around yourself and other people. Some of them are empowering, but most of them are limiting and they will be holding you back. If you're not aware of them, you can't possibly challenge them, which is why I've shared a number of exercises to help raise your awareness of your beliefs, and then challenge and reframe the ones that don't serve you. Doing this frees you from those limiting beliefs and opens up more possibilities in your life.

Another cornerstone I explored was values, which are the principles by which you live your life. These are the things that you believe are fundamentally important, and they influence your decisions whether you're aware of them or not. The section about values is designed to help you understand how they influence you, but more importantly I've also provided you with a tool that you can use to work out what your operational values are, how you can ensure they're met, and how you can use them to navigate uncertainty and conflict.

The combination of all of this insight is ultimately the second cornerstone of emotional and social intelligence: self-regulation (with the first cornerstone being self-awareness). I've included exercises and tools along the way to help you put this thinking into practice. Of course, I have many, many more exercises but the ones are included will at least start you off.

I closed the book with a section about stress and performance. This is an important element of the book, because although we strive to bring the best version of ourselves to whatever we do, we are not invincible. We build sustainable momentum by successfully accessing our inner resources to fuel performance. But we're all susceptible to setbacks and challenges which can lead us to succumb to stress, burnout, and anxiety.

This final section of the book is there to help you if you find yourself in an acute moment of stress, or suffering from ongoing stress that's unmanageable. I've explored what you can do and what habits you can bring into your life to diminish the amount of stress you're experiencing. I've also explained what happens when you're in flow and focus, and given you advice about how you can maintain that state so that you can continue to perform in the best possible way both for your business and within your life. I've given you an extensive toolkit in this chapter because we can all benefit from more varied ways to manage stress.

With each chapter, I've not only shown you how this applies to you as an individual but how it impacts the teams running our businesses. I've deliberately shared real stories from the work with clients to help bring to life the application of mental fitness to business. I also included the Unilever business case so you can see the true impact that is possible if we are willing to invest in this important topic.

This Is Just the Beginning …

Knowledge is just one part of this journey. It is not enough to know. As I mentioned earlier in the book, even if you've read 500 books about how to fly an aeroplane, I'm not going to get into a plane with you in the cockpit until you've practised and put that knowledge into action.

That is where the real work starts. Reading, learning, and researching can provide you with the information, but it does not make you a practitioner and it doesn't get you out of your comfort zone.

Where you'll really start to see everything I've talked about impact and enhance the quality of your life is when you're brave enough to use the tools I've shared with you regularly. If you have been thinking, acting, and feeling one way for 30 years, then reading this book once isn't going to undo that. You have to apply the tools, and you have to practise.

Is it hard? Yes! But just like the first time you go for a run or go to the gym and then ache the next day, the more often you do it the easier it becomes and the less you ache. Do you remember the neural pathways I talked about? Imagine a field of barley that has one path beaten through it. That was always the easiest path, but what you're trying to do now is create a new path through that field of barley. The first time you beat down that barley it's hard to see where the path is, it gets in your face, you want to backtrack and go the other way. But the first time is always the hardest.

The second time it's a little easier, the third time it's easier still, and before you know it, this new pathway is equal in terms of its ease, speed, and efficiency to the path you started with. Our neural pathways work the same way; don't be put off by difficulty you experience the first time you use the new pathway, as each time it will get easier and more habitual.

What I want to do via this book is help you create habits in your life – but you can't create habits by doing something once; you need to commit. You have to be committed, and through this commitment to practice, this will soon become a natural way of being for you.

All of the tools available within this book can also be downloaded from www.symbiapartners/mentalfitnessresources. Print them out and give them to your family, friends, and teammates. I would advise you to continuously revisit them and use them yourself. Now that you've read this book, don't leave it languishing on a shelf: pick it up and dip in and out of it whenever you need to.

If you encounter a situation and you can't remember what to do, dip into the book, go back to the relevant chapter, find the exercise, and use it to help improve your mental fitness.

Of course, reading and doing exercises is just one way of engaging with the topic of mental fitness. I have numerous ways of further engaging you and your people. At Symbia, we help companies, leaders, and teams to interact with this topic in a way that best works for them. Symbia was founded on a simple idea: that there's a direct, symbiotic relationship between our teams and ourselves, that our workplaces and our well-being are intertwined. Work is so much more than just a job – it's where we spend half our waking lives.

We specialise in leadership, capability building, team development, and unlocking performance through mental fitness, and we believe successful teams work best when each individual is equipped with the tools and techniques to realise their full potential.

We have a full Mental Fitness suite: we run 90-minute live webinar sessions; we have a 'self-serve' course; we offer 6- and 12-month programmes; we host two- and three-day live workshops, as well as train the trainer models so you can bring the know-how in-house.

We have options to cater for all possible needs, so if you are excited about the topic of mental fitness and want to bring it to your team or your business, please get in touch: team@symbiapartners.com.

INDEX